TOURING IN WINE COUNTRY

THE MOSEL & RHEINGAU

MITCHELL BEAZLEY

TOURING IN WINE COUNTRY

THE MOSEL & RHEINGAU

including The Ahr, Nahe and Pfalz

STUART PIGOTT

SERIES EDITOR

HUGH JOHNSON

Touring in Wine Country
The Mosel & Rheingau
published by Mitchell Beazley,
part of Reed Consumer Books Limited,
Michelin House, 81 Fulham Road,
London SW3 6RB
and Auckland, Melbourne, Singapore
and Toronto

First published in 1997

A CIP catalogue record of this book is
available from the British Library

ISBN 1 85732 8752

Editors: Jamie Ambrose, Susan Keevil
Senior Art Editor: Paul Drayson
Designer: Mark Richardson
Commissioning Editor: Sue Jamieson
Executive Art Editor: Fiona Knowles
Picture Research: Claire Gouldstone
Index: Angie Hipkin
Gazetteer: Sally Chorley
Production: Christina Quigley
Cartography: Map Creation Limited
and Lovell Johns Limited

Typeset in Bembo and Gill Sans
Origination by Mandarin Offset,
Singapore
Produced by Mandarin Offset
Printed and bound in Hong Kong

Contents

Maps

WEINKELLEREI
WEINGUT EXPORT

Keller's Keller
Gutsausschank

Foreword

Wine, more than anything else that we eat and drink, is resonant with the sense of place. Wines are formed by the ecology of their region, their soils and climates – but what shapes their character is a broader amalgam. The whole culture of region and country, all the cross-currents of history that form its taste and individuality, determine the kind of wine its people are accustomed to.

All these factors, from the geology underlying the land, the summer rain and spring frost, to the ruling dynasties of centuries ago, form part of the elusive concept of *terroir.* The richer the region and the longer its fields have been profitably cultivated the more they stamp their personality on their produce. Why are the world's most valuable wines those from vineyards with the longest consistent records? Because every generation, every decision by their owners, has contributed to their unique qualities. (This is not to say they cannot be mishandled to produce poor wine, but that their potential is the sum of their past and present.)

You can, of course, understand wine without being aware of its origin and roots. It would be underestimating our ancestors to say that because they may never have seen a vineyard they could not appreciate and memorize its character. But we are in the happy position of being able to trace our wine directly back to the trellises, cellars and families that shaped it. It is a journey anyone can make. We can eat the food that they eat with it: become as it were honorary members of the community and culture that forms it.

No wonder wine tourism is growing exponentially. Once you have discovered the hospitality of wine growers, their desire to share (amazingly, often with their rivals too) and the way the wine community spans the globe in friendly collaboration you will want to explore it all.

If there were a wine-country hospitality league, a contest for which region puts on the best show for the visitor, nowhere in Europe would compete with Germany for the friendly welcome, the ubiquitous flowery garden or cosy fire-side, or the range of open bottles to be sampled.

German wine-growers tend to be inn-keepers at heart, or at least to double as inn-keepers in their spare moments. Coupled with the beauty of the country they farm their open-door policy makes Germany (and I include Austria) the most enjoyable and accessible of all wine-lands.

It is the nature of German wine, too, to be light and easy to digest from the first morning glass to prolonged refreshment late at night.

This book celebrates and offers the key to the land of the Riesling, the origin and world headquarters of the greatest single white grape. Before you react with the challenge of Chardonnay let me ask you when you ever met a tingling apple-fresh Chardonnay of no more that 7% alcohol but intense and lingering flavours, a 40-year-old Chardonnay of creamy golden depth but still piquant and vital, or a Chardonnay like inspired honey with rich imitations of smoke and oranges. All these are easily within reach of the Riesling of the Mosel and the Rheingau. There is simply no other grape that offers this variety, added to, moreover, by the flavours of soil and situation that come through its limpid transparency with memorable force.

The Riesling came from the River Main east of Frankfurt to the Rheingau in the late Middle Ages. It made the fortune of this favoured range of hills sloping south to the Rhine. To this day almost nothing else is planted between the river and the hill-top forests, while its villages – many of opera-set prettiness, gabled, half-timbered and full of flowers – still have wine as their sole end and aim.

Germany's oldest inhabited house is here – now of course a wine-restaurant. The Rheingau is almost urban, intensely active: one of the most sophisticated wine-landscapes on earth. It bustles, like its river with its endless strings of barges perpetually passing to and fro.

The Mosel is different. The Riesling was implanted on the steepest vineyard slopes of all: there are places where you need a ladder to climb the hill. Vines alternate with forest and bare rock in rhythm with the great loops of the river: stacked on each south slope so densely that the medieval villages are almost pushed into the water. The Mosel has Trier, too, the capital of Roman Gaul and still dense with Roman remains.

The Palatinate occupies the place of Alsace in the hierarchy of German vineyards. Like Alsace it is a place of gastronomic enterprise, with some of the country's best cooking evolving round a dynamic wine industry. Between Rheingau and Palatinate lie the Nahe and Rheinhessen, each interpreting the Riesling in its own way, and adding its own grape specialities to enrich what is already one of Europe's richest wine-touring regions.

Hugh Johnson

Introduction

For untold centuries, visitors have been awestruck by the natural drama of the Rhine and Mosel valleys. Vines have been an inextricable part of this landscape since at least the fourth century AD, when the Roman poet Ausonius wrote the first surviving description of it in his poem *Mosella*. Twisting rivers, steep-sided valleys, rolling hills, medieval castles and Roman ruins, cliffs and glistening streams… the scene is ever-changing, save for the constant presence of vineyards. Here vines flourish on lofty, narrow terraces and slopes so precipitous that it makes you dizzy even to look up at them from flat ground.

The marriage of natural severity and abundance gives the Rhine and Mosel valleys their unique fascination. The same can be said of these regions' wines, in which richness is matched by delicacy, and extrovert fruit interwoven with crisp acidity to create a scintillating whole. No other wines reflect their landscape more precisely than these. Today's wines are the result of centuries of experimentation begun by the Romans, continued by monks throughout the Middle Ages and Renaissance, and carried to fruition by the aristocracy and landed gentry during the 19th century. During recent years a new generation of young winemakers without titles or imposing residences have taken this process of refinement even further.

Today, as over the last two centuries, the finest German wines are Rieslings made from late-picked grapes which retain a touch of natural grape sweetness. Modern winemaking methods, which have given producers more control over fermentation, have enabled leading estates to perfect this style of wine, and have also opened the doors to a sea of generic Rhine and Mosel wines often described, quite fairly, as 'sugar-water'.

Over the last 10 years, the standard of the dry wines has dramatically improved. The demand for balanced wines has

Left *Lorchhausen, in the Rheingau. Vines have grown here for generations: both on the terraces that flank the town – broad steps like these now replacing traditional narrow ledges – and decorating its gardens* (above).

Wine Regions of Germany

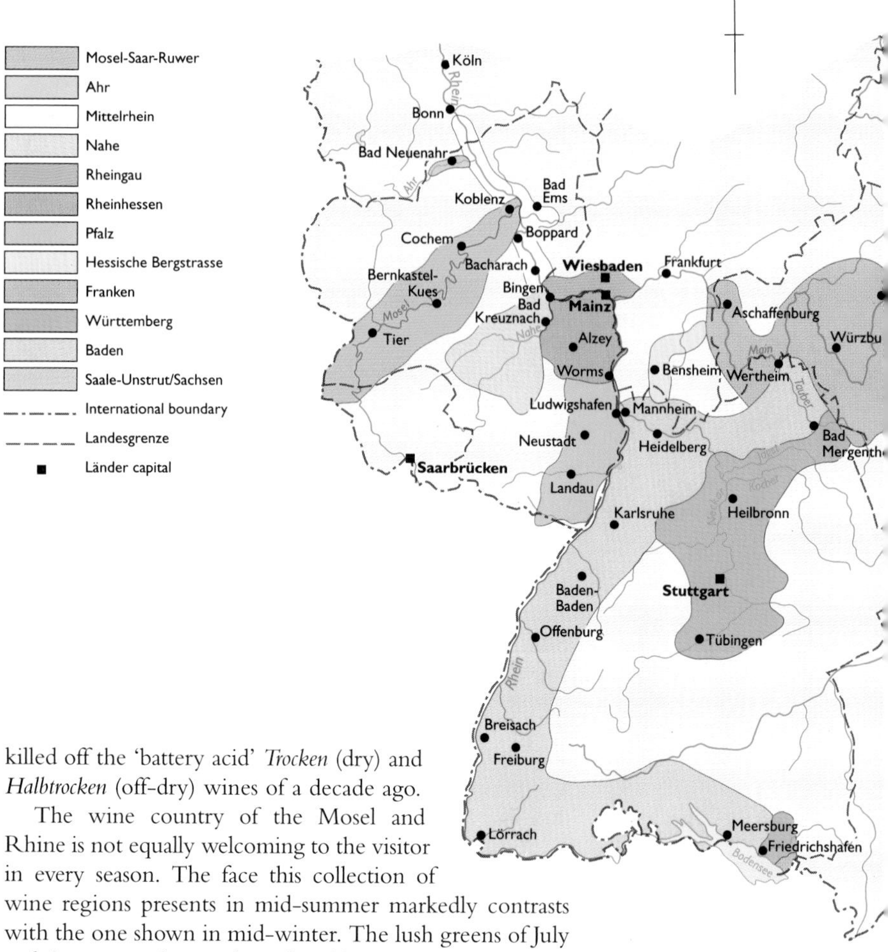

killed off the 'battery acid' *Trocken* (dry) and *Halbtrocken* (off-dry) wines of a decade ago.

The wine country of the Mosel and Rhine is not equally welcoming to the visitor in every season. The face this collection of wine regions presents in mid-summer markedly contrasts with the one shown in mid-winter. The lush greens of July and August are frequently replaced by a blanket of snow in January and February. During the spring and autumn, the driving rain can change to brilliant sunshine within minutes.

The natural beauty and architectural richness of these regions means that their most famous towns and villages have become popular destinations with day-trippers and holiday-makers as well as the wine tourist. Because of this, careful planning is necessary to avoid the crowds during peak season.

There has been a revolution in the German restaurant scene over the last 20 years, its restaurants now have more Michelin stars than any country save France, though change has not reached every region. Great wines and great food do not always coincide, which is another reason why a detailed guide such as this is important for the wine traveller in Germany.

Left *A Burg, or castle, rises over Bernkastel, displaying the fine architectural style that typifies the region and accentuates its ever-present natural beauty*

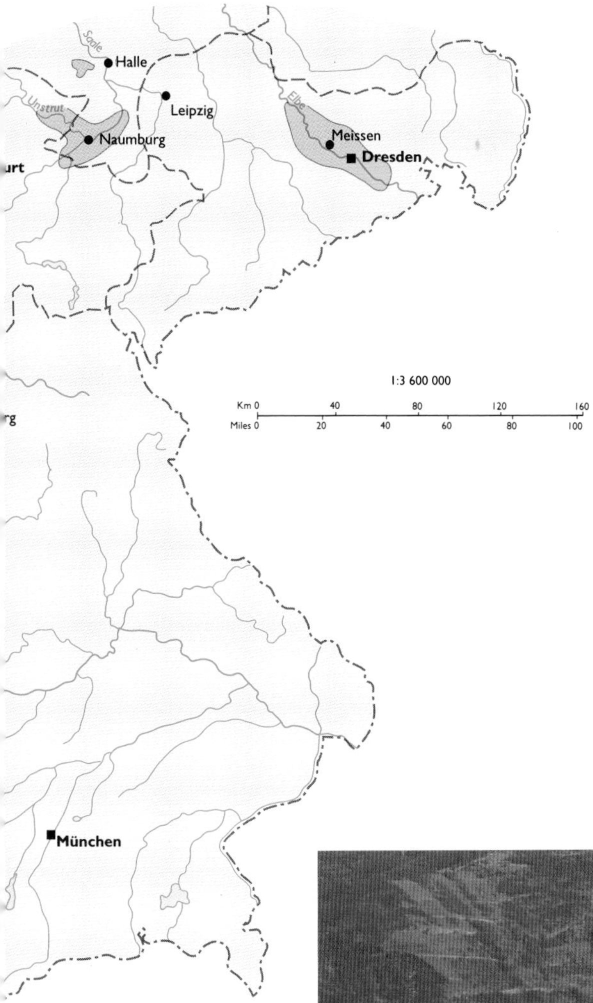

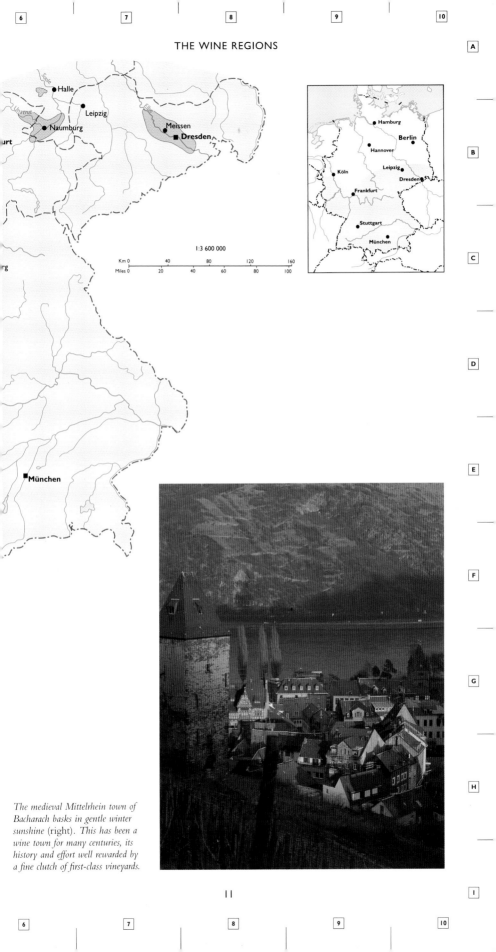

The medieval Mittelrhein town of Bacharach basks in gentle winter sunshine (right). This has been a wine town for many centuries, its history and effort well rewarded by a fine clutch of first-class vineyards.

Landscape and climate

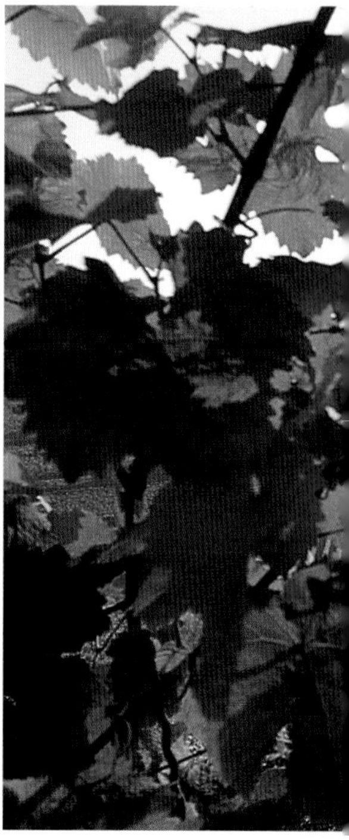

For more than a decade, 'cool-climate viticulture' has been a catch-phrase for winemakers from South Australia to South Africa, from New York State to New Zealand. Throughout the New World it stands for wines with fresh fruit flavours, subtle aromas and an elegant balance of the wine's constituent elements. In fact, the natural beginnings of cool-climate viticulture took place more than 1,600 years ago, when the Romans planted vines in the cool river valleys of northwestern Germany. They knew that the hill country there was too inhospitable for wine-growing, however, and therefore selected sites with the most favourable microclimates. This led them to sheltered pockets in the steep-sided river valleys that cut deep into the hills. By the fourth century AD, they had planted significant areas of vineyard in many of the sites that continue to be regarded as Germany's top vineyards.

The combination of a cool general climate and an amenable microclimate (which allows the sun's warmth to be caught and stored by river water and rock) is the basis

With more than 25,000 hectares of vines, Rheinhessen (left) *is the largest wine-growing region in the whole of Germany. Wines produced here tend to be as diverse in style as the vineyards themselves.*

for all the great German wines. The microclimates of the Rhine and Mosel valleys, together with late-ripening grapes, lead to an extremely long growing season. Typically, it takes around 120 days from flowering until the harvest, but depending upon conditions, this figure can extend to 150 days' ripening on the vine. Further south, late harvesting can result in fat, overblown wines, but here it means wines that are simply packed with fruit flavours and aromas.

The typical pattern of autumn weather (mist in the early morning, which lets in brilliant sunshine by noon) greatly encourages the development of *botrytis*, or 'noble rot'. Noble rot is an essential factor in some of Germany's greatest beverages: the luscious *Beerenauslese* and *Trockenbeerenauslese* dessert wines. When this fungus infects fully ripe grapes under the right weather conditions, the berries shrivel and their contents undergo a complex and beneficial chemical transformation. The hard frosts which frequently follow the end of the main harvest ensure that another local speciality possible: *Eiswein*. 'Ice wine' is made from grapes picked and pressed while frozen; the result is intensely sweet wine with an almost electric tension between richness and acidity. The best of these are among the most expensive young wines in the world.

The different climates of the regions covered in this book strongly influence the styles of wine produced. For example, in the warmest region – the Pfalz – it is possible to produce dry wines with 13 percent alcohol in good vintages. In the coolest, the Mosel-Saar-Ruwer, many of the finest wines will not ferment to more than a slight seven percent alcohol. Soil type complicates the picture even further. The stony, acidic, grey-slate soil of the Mosel Valley, for example, accentuates the sleekness and crispness of its Riesling wines. Take some time to study the wines in the regions in which they grow, and it quickly becomes apparent that Germany's greatest wines are no less strongly influenced by the soil and microclimate than those of France.

Left *The famous Nierstein vineyard: its warm climate is ideal for ripening the luscious Rieslings that originally gave it fame.*

Above *The old village of Cochem: the long, gentle growing seasons and distinctive slate soils here are what give Mosel wines their typical sleekness.*

Grape varieties

It is no accident that **Riesling** is the most important grape variety for quality wines in all the viticultural regions along the Rhine and Mosel. It is the grape best able to take advantage of the cool climate and rapidly changing weather conditions – weather conditions that pose problems for other grapes, but give Riesling wines the elegance and aromatic complexity that make fine German wine unique.

The Riesling grape is also sensitive to the smallest differences in microclimate and soil. This expresses itself in Riesling wine's enormous spectrum of aromas, ranging from green apple to peach, blackcurrant to pineapple, dill to aniseed, and all kinds of mineral notes. The minerally character of top-class German Rieslings is intense, yet enigmatic; you have to experience a fine Mosel Riesling to really understand what the 'slatey' character of these wines smells and tastes like.

Today, the most important noble white grapes besides Riesling are Pinot Blanc and Pinot Gris – in German, **Weissburgunder** and **Grauburgunder** respectively. Even

Top and top right *Spätburgunder grapes, known as Pinot Noir to the rest of the world. Past problems with this variety turned out to be due to bad winemaking; today, German reds are beginning to be compared with those of Burgundy's Côte d'Or – and the Pfalz is leading the way among the regions.*

in the Mosel-Saar-Ruwer, where Riesling is king of quality wines, Weissburgunder has established a serious foothold. Both grapes yield medium-bodied, dry whites that are easier-drinking than young, dry Rieslings: the reason for their considerable success at home and abroad. However, only in the Pfalz do they sometimes scale the heights of quality these grapes regularly reach in the warmer climates of Baden and Alsace.

Weiss- and Grauburgunder have also been stealing the march on **Silvaner**, once the second-string grape of the Rhine regions. Now, only in the hill country of Rheinhessen, does it have a significant future. Here dessert wines from the **Huxelrebe** grape are a rarity well worth seeking out. Further south in the Pfalz, the aromatic grapes **Gewürztraminer**, **Muskateller** (Muscat à Petits Grains) and **Scheurebe** can give magnificent dry and dessert wines, but remain specialities.

The downside is the long list of modern grapes that are cultivated for the mass-production of generic wines. **Müller-Thurgau** is the most important of these high-yielding vines which generally give soft wines that are supposed to be slightly spicy, but are just as frequently neutral. At least with modest yields Müller-Thurgau can be persuaded to yield appealingly supple, dry whites. The same cannot be said of grapes from modern vine-crossings such as Ortega, Optima and Siegerrebe, which deserve to land in the dustbin of wine history.

While Germany is primarily a white-wine nation, red grapes account for 18.5 percent of the vineyard area. In the Middle Ages this figure was much higher, but the success of white wines in the 19th and 20th centuries greatly reduced the area planted with red grapes. After having made only thin, pale wines from **Spätburgunder** or Pinot Noir, some serious red wines have been produced in the last decade. Not surprisingly, the warmest of the Rhine regions, the Pfalz, is the leader here, beginning to measure up to the Burgundian ideal, and also becoming a source of simple reds for everyday drinking made from the modern **Dornfelder** grape.

Above left *Gewürztraminer, as its name suggests, produces a spicy, aromatic wine – here in Germany more delicate and elegant in style than its Alsace counterpart.*
Above *The Silvaner grape is less well-loved these days, expressing its best only in the confines of selected Rheinhessen vineyards.*

Vineyard classification

Not surprisingly in a climate like northern Germany's, where the smallest differences in vineyard exposure have a direct and dramatic influence on wine quality, the names of the best vineyards have long since gained high reputations. Two hundred years ago, the wines from great vineyards in the Rhine and Mosel regions, such as the Marcobrunn, Rüdesheimer Berg, Scharzhofberg and Brauneberg, were already highly prized. Until the 1920s, they were the most expensive wines in the world, outpricing even the premier Grand Cru Classé of Bordeaux.

The classifications of France are famous worldwide, while those of Germany are only just being rediscovered. It is a little-known fact that the Prussians undertook the world's first scientifically surveyed official vineyard classification in the Mosel-Saar-Ruwer between 1816 and 1832, publishing the results in map form in 1868. Unfortunately, present German wine law is based on a different principal chosen for reasons of political expediency. It makes the sugar-content of the grapes at harvest the sole criterion for wine quality.

In the climate of northern Germany, five pickings from a single-vineyard site during the harvest can result in five wines ranging from the light and dry to the lusciously sweet. Since the introduction of selective harvesting in Germany 200 years ago, the tradition has been to bottle

Above *Young Nierstein vines with plenty of space between rows to allow the passage of vineyard machinery.*

Right *Autumn vines in the Ahr: close-planted vineyards like this one usually give better quality wine.*

Above *Riesling breaking into bud. Despite the prowess of other varieties, this is still the main grape associated with quality in all the Rhine regions.*

Left *Careful tending of the vines throughout the vintage and selective hand picking of the fruit – or even berries – at harvest time gives the very best quality* Prädikat *wines.*

wines separately, grading them according to their richness and sophistication. The *Prädikat* system of wine grading now enshrined in the German wine law is in ascending order as follows: *Kabinett*, *Spätlese*, *Auslese*, *Beerenauslese/Eiswein*, *Trockenbeerenauslese*. It worked well as long as it was confined to noble grapes varieties. Sadly, though, today's wine law's obsession with grape sugar, together with new grape varieties bred for their ability to produce sugar rather than flavour, has resulted in chaos. Spätlese, for example, appears on the labels of some of Germany's finest wines, and on the labels of many cheap, characterless wines.

For the majority of Germany's leading wine producers, vineyard classification is the only logical way out of this mess. Many have already introduced stringent internal classifications. Most now limit the use of vineyard names to the Prädikat wines from the top sites, selling their regular-quality wines (*Qualitätswein/Tafelwein*) under the name of the estate – for example, Fritz Haag Riesling or Karl H Johner Weissburgunder. In various regions there are campaigns to incorporate vineyard classifications into wine law. The Rheingau is the closest to success with its 1997 vintage earmarked for the top German wine classification, *Erstes Gewächs*. However, as is usual with red tape, the appropriate amendment to the wine law has yet to be passed by the State of Hessen parliament.

Viticulture and winemaking

In Germany, styles of vine-growing range from the ancient to the hyper-modern. In the Middle Mosel large areas of vineyard are still planted in the Roman style, each vine trained against its own pole with only one metre separating the vines. With old, ungrafted vines this ancient system produces some of the greatest Rieslings. The modern vineyards of the Rhine regions, where the vines are trained high on wires to give leaves and grapes the best exposure to daylight and air, represent the other extreme. New World winemakers have only recently discovered this kind of viticulture, and have christened it 'canopy management'.

Different systems of cultivation have important implications for the vintner and, indirectly, for consumers. The production costs for a top-quality Mosel Riesling can be up to 10 times higher than those for a Müller-Thurgau mechanically cultivated from vineyards in the Rheinhessen or the Pfalz. The cost of labour is one reason for this enormous difference; yields is the other. Today, Germany's first-rank producers take yields as low as their colleagues in Burgundy. While others would like to follow suit, they are unable to sell their wines at commercially viable prices.

One of the most costly operations in winemaking is hand-picking grapes, essential in all steep vineyards. This is also the only way to selectively harvest: either to exclude poor grapes, or to separate nobly-rotten grapes for Auslese and higher Prädikat wines. It is an arduous business, especially

The Rheingau's Kloster Eberbach (above) *is synonymous with wine. By the 14th century, the monks here were the largest commercial producers of wine in the world.*

on a one-in-four slope with the temperature hovering just above zero! Excellent organization and great determination are necessary for success.

The first principal followed by Germany's leading white-wine producers is: do as little as possible, but as much as absolutely necessary. Gentle pressing of the grapes is usually followed by natural settling of the juice (12 to 48 hours). The wine then flows into neutral oak casks or stainless-steel tanks for fermentation. Today, this rarely lasts for fewer than three or four weeks, and in the cold cellars of the Mosel it can easily last three or four months. A single filtration prior to spring bottling is ideal, since handling the wine too much will detract from its flavour.

Once, German red wines were made virtually like white wines; today, the best use almost identical methods to red burgundy: fermentation on the skins for two to three weeks, pressing, then maturation in new oak *barriques* (225- to 300-litre new-oak casks) for between one and two years. Bottling without filtration is increasingly practised. While top Rieslings from the Mosel and Rhine come very close to realising the full potential of the great vineyards here, the Spätburgunder red wines of the Pfalz still have some way to go.

Left *The steepness of this Urzig vineyard in the Mosel means that each vine needs to be supported by its own pole – with no training wires, this makes getting about the vineyard easier too.*

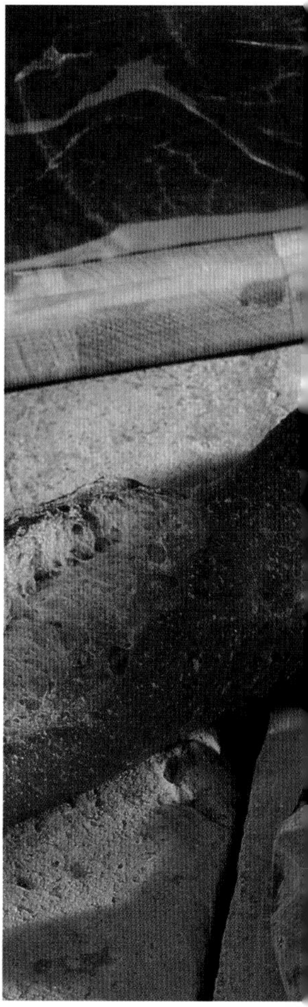

Cuisine

Germany has undergone an extraordinary culinary revolution over the last 20 years; you only have to glance at the star-studded maps in the German edition of the Michelin guide to recognise this. Excellent restaurants can now be found almost everywhere, and the country's top chefs need fear no comparisons with their most famous colleagues across the border in France. This is not the entire picture, however. Ordinary Germans still do not have an appreciation of food comparable to that of the French or northern Italians. In the 'wrong' region in Germany, you can still often end up with a big piece of fatty pork on your plate swimming in a crude, glutinous sauce.

Perhaps it is because this clichéed image of German cooking is thoroughly etched into the collective consciousness that many of its great specialities are unknown to foreigners. Many visitors are, for example, completely unaware of the delights of *Spargel* (white asparagus). For them, asparagus is merely a green vegetable served with salmon, rather than a dish in itself, or accompanied by potatoes and sliced ham, or a small steak, as it is in Germany. Some of Germany's best white asparagus comes from Ingelheim, in Rheinhessen, and from the Pfalz. The asparagus season, which lasts from April until June 20, is another reason to visit the region in the spring. Dry Weissburgunder or Riesling Kabinett (not too dry) is ideal with Spargel. The dry Silvaner that is usually recommended is often too sour to make a good match.

Also new for many visitors are the wild mushrooms: *Pfifferlinge* (chantarelles) in summer and *Steinpilzen* (ceps/porcini) in late summer and autumn. They can be served in many different ways, the classic combinations being *Pfifferlinge mit Semmelknödel* (in a cream sauce with bread dumplings), and *Steinpilzen mit Kalbsmilch* (with veal sweetbreads; sometimes called *Kalbsbries*). The former is perfect with a full-bodied, dry Riesling from the Rhine

Top left *The clean-up of Germany's rivers has resulted in an ever-growing demand for fish of all types, including eel and pike.*
Above *For simple fare, particularly on picnics, one could do worse than a plate of Schinken und Salat – ham and salad – and, of course, a glass of wine.*

Wild mushrooms (right) *abound in modern German cuisine, including* Pfifferlinge *(chanterelles) and* Steinpilzen *(ceps).*

and the latter is heavenly with a slightly sweet Riesling Spätlese/Auslese from either the Mosel or the Nahe.

The clean-up of Germany's rivers has caused a renaissance of interest in river fish, such as *Hecht* (pike) and *Aal* (eel), and lake fish such as *Zander* (pike-perch). All need careful preparation, Hecht due to its bones, Zander due to its delicate flavour, and Aal due to its oiliness. And all demand dry wines. With Riesling, look for Trocken/Charta wines that are at least two years old, or a young dry Weissburgunder/Grauburgunder. Smoked eel, like other smoked fish, is perfect with Mosel Riesling Kabinett wines that are on the sweet, rather than dry, side.

Game is no less of a surprise. The forests close to the vineyards of the Rhine and Mosel valleys are full of *Wildschwein* (wild boar), *Reh* (roe deer) and *Hirsch* (stag). *Hase* (hare) and *Wild'ente* (wild duck) are also relatively common. These are meats that are equally complemented by the best Spätburgunder red wines and mature Riesling Spätlese/Auslese with natural sweetness (not dry).

Of course, German bread (*Brot*), sausage (*Wurst*) and ham (*Schinken*) should not be forgotten when planning a picnic.

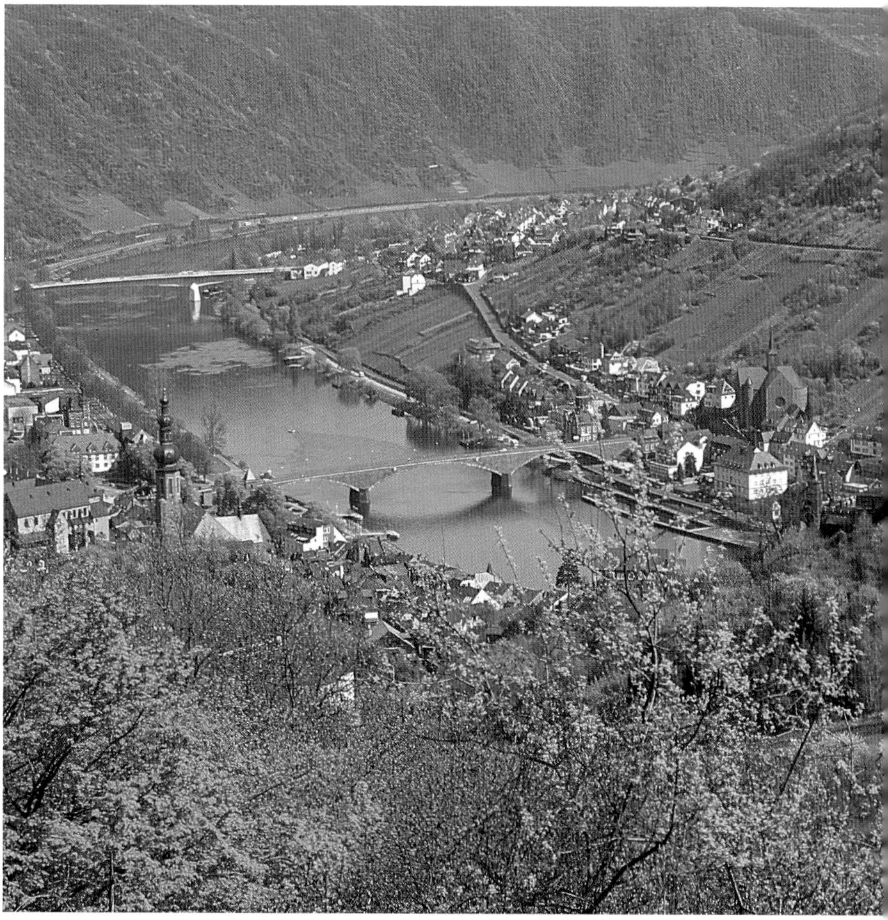

How to use this guide

This book is designed to help travellers who wish to write their own itineraries as well as those who want guidance every step of the way. It provides a route, or series of routes, through the heart of each wine region. Follow one fully, including visits to estates, and it will take up the better part of a day, though it naturally depends on your exact starting point.

The most convenient starting point for tours to the regions covered in this book are Trier (nearest airport, Luxembourg) for the Mosel-Saar-Ruwer, and Frankfurt (nearest airport Frankfurt/Main) for the Rhine regions.

The stunning landscape of the Mosel Valley (above) *is a must for anyone seeking both wines and dramatic courntryside. Fascinating architectural features and intriguing towns are no less abundant.*

VISITING ESTATES

Winemakers in Germany usually love talking about their wines and tasting them with interested visitors. However, when planning a trip to the Rhine and Mosel it is worth remembering that most of the best wines are produced by small, family-run estates. If possible, ring to make appointments in advance, or you might find that nobody is there

to receive you. When travelling, try to remember that turning up late for an appointment can be worse than not having one. A short call to report delays is always appreciated. Nearly all the producers featured in this guide speak very good English.

The harvest is an extremely stressful time for wine-growers. In the south, the quality-wine harvest typically gets under way during the latter part of September and continues into the second half of October. On the Mosel, it usually does not begin until mid-October and continues into early November. During this period wine-growers may still receive visitors, but will not have much time to spare.

Large estates are set up to receive visitors without appointment, and there is no need to buy anything – though it will be appreciated if you do. With smaller estates it is discourteous to take up a wine-grower's time and not take something with you.

The thumbnail sketches of producers included aim to give an overview of all the important estates within the areas covered by the maps, and many just outside their scope. In the Mosel and Rhine regions, the best place to buy wine is almost invariably the estates themselves; sadly, good wine stores are rare. Extensive selections of fine German wines can be found at FUB (Feggers, Unterberg & Berts) in Cologne, and Weinland-Keiler in Dortmund and Neu-Isenburg (near Frankfurt).

HOTELS

Hotel recommendations have been made on a similar basis to restaurant recommendations (*see* below).

RESTAURANTS

Suggestions for eating out focus on the best restaurants and moderately priced places that serve good, rustic food. Beware unlisted establishments in touristy towns and villages.

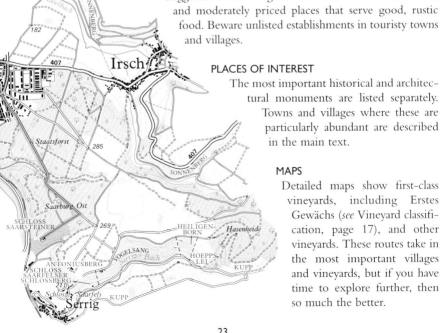

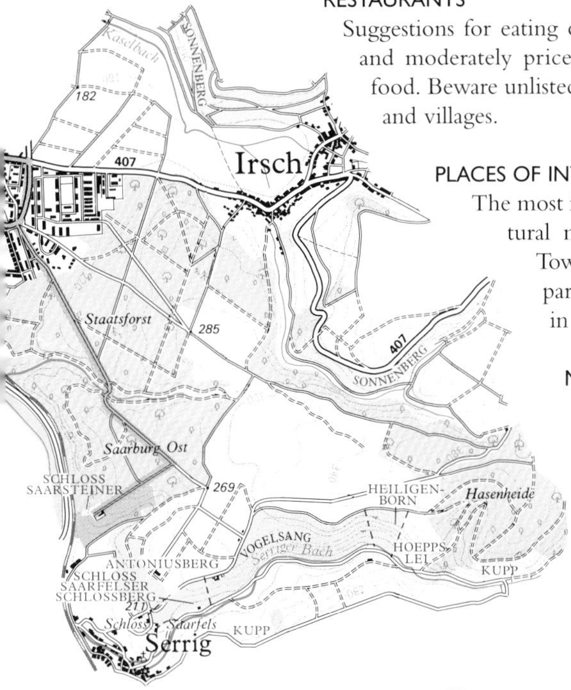

PLACES OF INTEREST

The most important historical and architectural monuments are listed separately. Towns and villages where these are particularly abundant are described in the main text.

MAPS

Detailed maps show first-class vineyards, including Erstes Gewächs (*see* Vineyard classification, page 17), and other vineyards. These routes take in the most important villages and vineyards, but if you have time to explore further, then so much the better.

Königsbacher

Trier and environs

Any tour of the Mosel naturally begins at or passes through Trier, Germany's oldest city. In spite of its innumerable Roman, medieval and Baroque monuments, Trier is much more than a vast museum, bubbling over with all aspects of modern life. Today, as in centuries past, the *Hauptmarkt*, or main marketplace, forms the bustling centre of the city as well as acting as a showcase for virtually all its architectural styles. Almost everything of interest in the *Altstadt* (Old Town) is within easy walking distance.

Trier was founded in 16AD by the Emperor Augustus. By the fourth century, it was the largest city north of Alps, and the effective capital of the Roman Empire during its latter years. You don't have to look far for signs of this former glory. The Porta Nigra, the largest surviving Roman gatehouse in the world; the Basilika, originally the Emperor Constantine's *Palastaula* or throne-room; and the *Dom* (cathedral), begun in 325AD, survive in an astonishing state of preservation. The imposing ruins of the amphitheatre and imperial baths also bear witness to Trier's Roman grandeur and political importance. Archaeologists from the *Landesmuseum*, or regional museum, uncover more of the city's history every year, and it is seldom that a dig is not in progress somewhere. A wealth of these discoveries is displayed in the museum.

Trier also has a subterranean aspect. Three of the Mosel-Saar-Ruwer's largest wine estates have cavernous cellars here; at the Bischöfliche Weingüter, for example, they are so extensive that the cellarmaster travels around by bicycle, while at the Vereinigte Hospitien, one underground gallery dates back to Roman times. Romans introduced winemaking to the region and established their central winery here, so Trier can claim nearly 2,000 years of winemaking tradition.

From the departure of the Romans until the Napoleonic secularization during the first years of the 19th century, the

Trier offers sites of almost every architectural style, not least around the Hauptmarkt (left and above): this is the old city centre, still one of the best and most accessible starting places for a full exploration of the city.

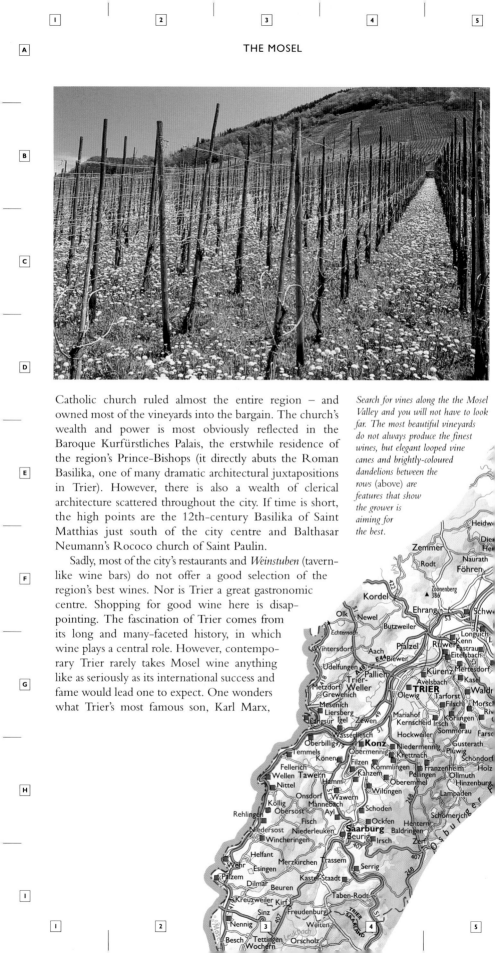

Catholic church ruled almost the entire region – and owned most of the vineyards into the bargain. The church's wealth and power is most obviously reflected in the Baroque Kurfürstliches Palais, the erstwhile residence of the region's Prince-Bishops (it directly abuts the Roman Basilika, one of many dramatic architectural juxtapositions in Trier). However, there is also a wealth of clerical architecture scattered throughout the city. If time is short, the high points are the 12th-century Basilika of Saint Matthias just south of the city centre and Balthasar Neumann's Rococo church of Saint Paulin.

Sadly, most of the city's restaurants and *Weinstuben* (tavern-like wine bars) do not offer a good selection of the region's best wines. Nor is Trier a great gastronomic centre. Shopping for good wine here is disappointing. The fascination of Trier comes from its long and many-faceted history, in which wine plays a central role. However, contemporary Trier rarely takes Mosel wine anything like as seriously as its international success and fame would lead one to expect. One wonders what Trier's most famous son, Karl Marx,

Search for vines along the the Mosel Valley and you will not have to look far. The most beautiful vineyards do not always produce the finest wines, but elegant looped vine canes and brightly-coloured dandelions between the rows (above) are features that show the grower is aiming for the best.

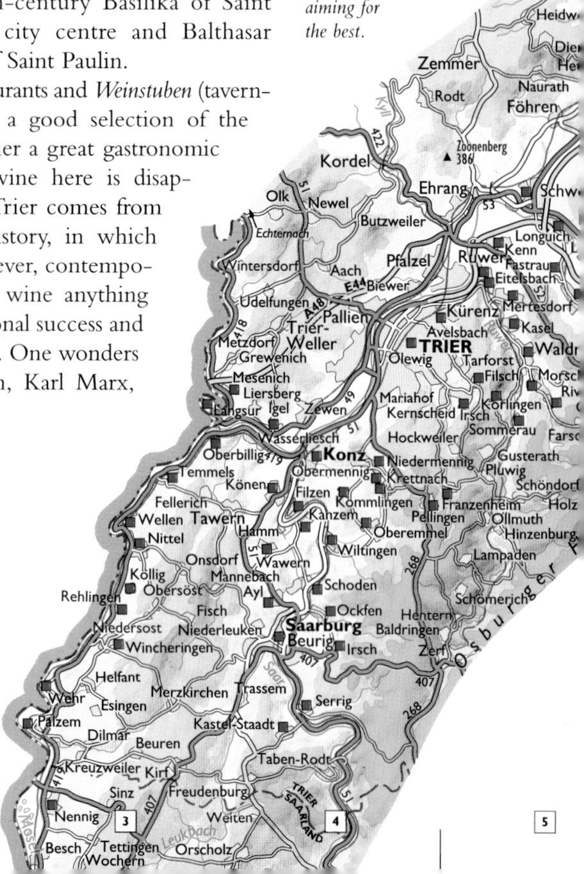

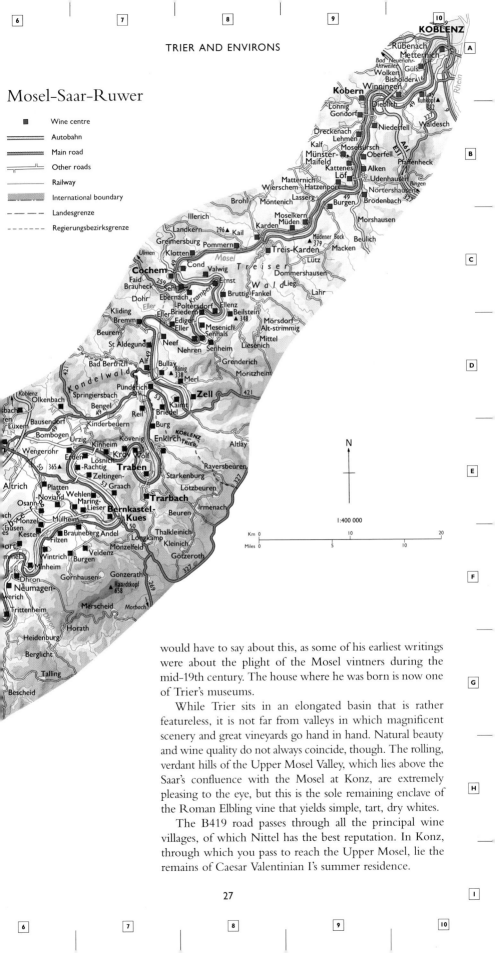

would have to say about this, as some of his earliest writings were about the plight of the Mosel vintners during the mid-19th century. The house where he was born is now one of Trier's museums.

While Trier sits in an elongated basin that is rather featureless, it is not far from valleys in which magnificent scenery and great vineyards go hand in hand. Natural beauty and wine quality do not always coincide, though. The rolling, verdant hills of the Upper Mosel Valley, which lies above the Saar's confluence with the Mosel at Konz, are extremely pleasing to the eye, but this is the sole remaining enclave of the Roman Elbling vine that yields simple, tart, dry whites.

The B419 road passes through all the principal wine villages, of which Nittel has the best reputation. In Konz, through which you pass to reach the Upper Mosel, lie the remains of Caesar Valentinian I's summer residence.

TRIER AND ENVIRONS

RECOMMENDED PRODUCERS

Reichsgraf von Kesselstatt
Liebfrauenstrasse 9–10
D 54920 Trier
Tel: (0651) 75101
One of the best large estates in Germany making a wide range of rich, aromatic Rieslings from the Middle Mosel, Saar and Ruwer. Tastings by appointment only.

Bischöfliche Weingüter
Gervasiusstrasse 1
D 54290 Trier
Tel: (0651) 43441
An association of three church estates sharing cellars and administration. Produces an enormous range of dependable light, fresh wines. By appointment only, closed weekends.

Vereinigte Hospitien
Krahnenufer 19
D 54290 Trier
Tel: (0651) 468210
Erratic wine quality, but magnificent cellars. By appointment only.

Friedrich-Wilhelm-Gymnasium
Weberbach 75
D 54290 Trier
Tel: (0651) 978300
Makes simple, light wines mainly from the Middle Mosel. Has its own wine shop, open standard hours.

HOTELS

Eurener Hof
D 54294 Trier-Euren
Tel: (0651) 88077
Attractive, quiet and moderately priced hotel located 3km from the centre of Trier.

Europa Parkhotel (Ramada)
Kaiserstrasse 29
D 54290 Trier
Tel: (0651) 71950
The most comfortable of the luxury hotels in the city centre, with prices to match.

RESTAURANTS

Landhaus Mühlenberg
Mühlenberg 2
D 54313 Daufenbach
Tel: (06505) 8779
The Stoebe family's fine restaurant is situated 12km outside Trier in a wooded valley. Modern cooking of a high standard and a good wine list.

Restaurant Scheid
Reinigerstrasse 48
D 54332 Wasserliesche
Tel: (06501) 13958
On a good day, mercurial Hubert Scheid is the Trier area's best chef. The wine list is sensational (Mosel and France). Also simple hotel rooms. 12km from Trier.

On the opposite bank of the Mosel lies an even more imposing Roman monument, the 23-metre-high Pillar of Igel. Igel itself lies on the B49 just outside Trier. Continue on this road to Oberbillig to reach the idyllic valley of the Sauer. While there is little wine-growing here, there is some of the most beautiful country in the region.

For wine tourists, the tributaries of the Mosel of greatest interest are the River Saar, converging with the Mosel at Konz, nine kilometres southwest of Trier, and the Ruwer, a stream which flows into the Mosel five kilometres northeast of the city. The wines made here perhaps best express the unique qualities of German wine as a whole. In poor vintages they are lean and acidic; in great vintages they take the interplay of ripeness and freshness, fruit and acidity – German Riesling's hallmark – to sublime heights.

It is worth noting that travelling from one valley to the other is more time-consuming than it looks on the map. Excellent navigation is necessary so as not to get lost on the back roads; the only alternative is going through Trier. It is best to play it safe and allow nearly an hour for this journey. Remember: rush-hour traffic can be heavy in Trier.

Below *Trier's clerical architecture presents itself in an abundance of different forms and in many different places. This statue guards the Vereinigte Hospitien, its guise little suggests the cavernous cellars beneath it built for wine storage.*

Above top *The Kurfürstliches Palais – not only Trier's most splendid illustration of Baroque architecture, but a reflection of the wealth and power of the church here.*

Above *Trier was once capital of the Roman Empire and there is little better evidence of this than the majestic Porta Nigra – the world's largest surviving Roman gatehouse.*

Restaurant Pfeffermühle
Zurlaubener Ufer 76
D 54292 Trier
Tel: (0651) 26133
The best restaurant within Trier. Specializes in classic French and German cooking and has a fine wine list (Mosel and France).

Kupfer-Pfanne
Ehranger Strasse 200
D 54293 Trier-Ehrang
Tel: (0651) 66589
Reliable, unpretentious restaurant situated 8km from central Trier. Good value for money.

Robert (auf der Festung)
Maximinstrasse 30
D 54340 Longuich
Tel: (06502) 4920
Erratic cooking (though good fish and game) that is less impressive than the architecture. Located 13km north of Trier.

Palais Kesselstatt
Liebfrauenstrasse 10
D 54290 Trier
Tel: (0651) 40204
Go for the simpler dishes at this slightly pretentious restaurant, located next door to the Kesselstatt estate in Trier.

Restaurant zum Domstein
Hauptmarkt 5
D 54290 Trier
Tel: (0651) 74490
This restaurant has an attractive courtyard. Rather dull German cooking but a good list of local wines (ask for the full list). Also, by prior arrangement, Roman-style food.

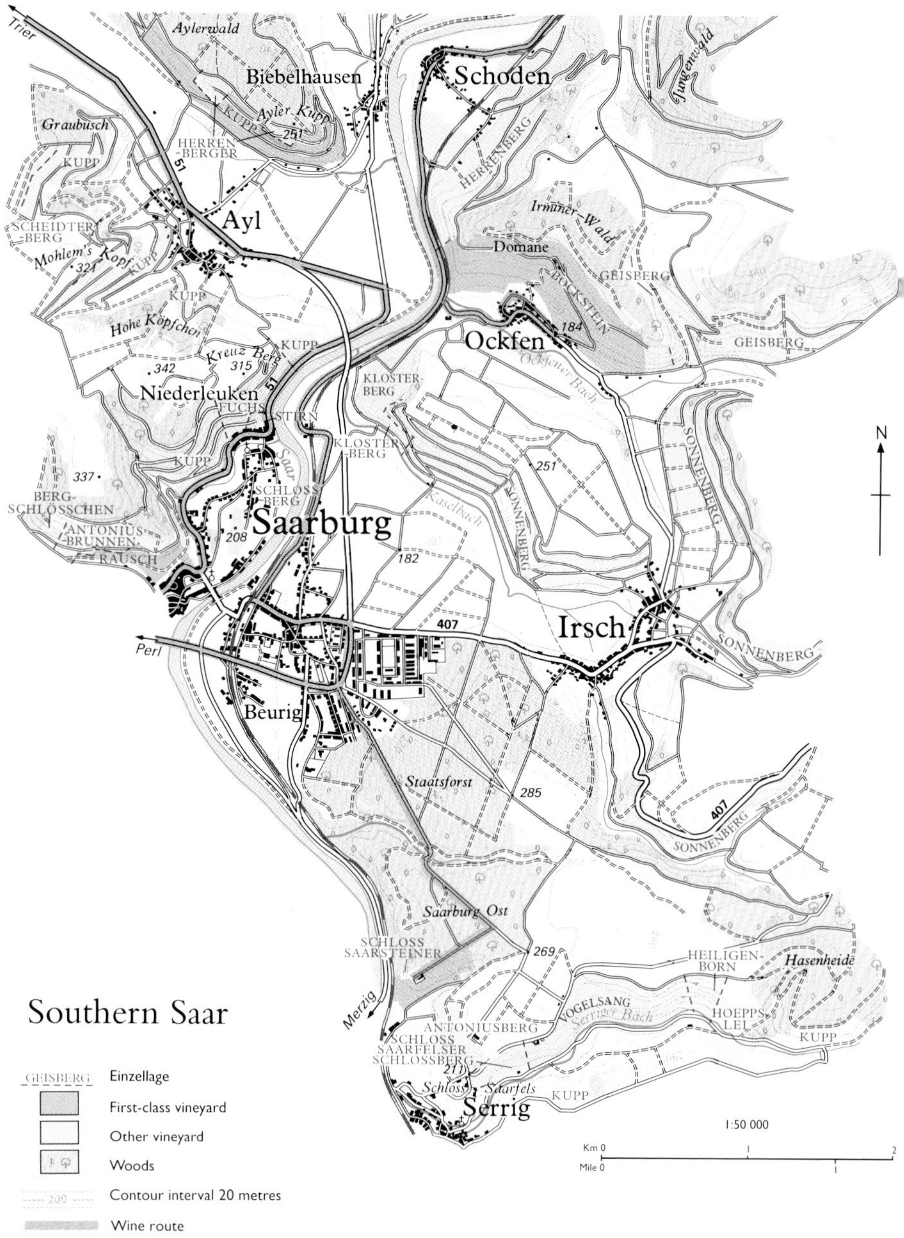

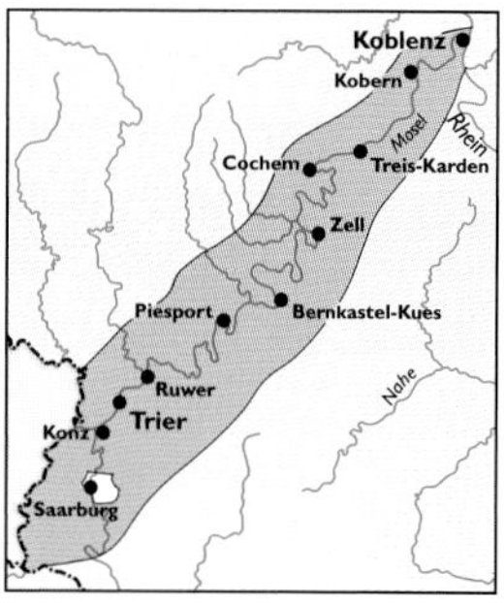

SAARBURG

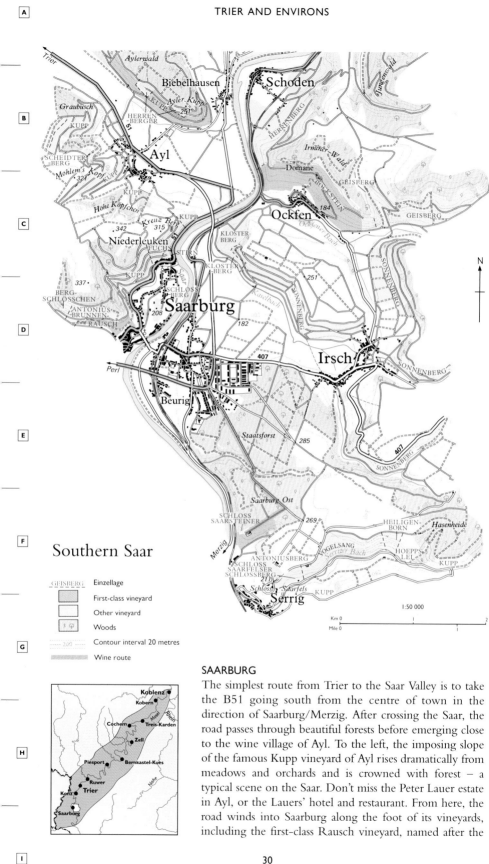

The simplest route from Trier to the Saar Valley is to take the B51 going south from the centre of town in the direction of Saarburg/Merzig. After crossing the Saar, the road passes through beautiful forests before emerging close to the wine village of Ayl. To the left, the imposing slope of the famous Kupp vineyard of Ayl rises dramatically from meadows and orchards and is crowned with forest – a typical scene on the Saar. Don't miss the Peter Lauer estate in Ayl, or the Lauers' hotel and restaurant. From here, the road winds into Saarburg along the foot of its vineyards, including the first-class Rausch vineyard, named after the

Left *Saarburg is a town for climbing: built on a rocky headland by the River Saar, the Altstadt boasts both a fortified tower and a beautiful chapel at the top of its high headland. But if you'd rather look up than climb up, the roaring Leukbach waterfall can be found in the old city too.*

Below *Okfen's pride and joy is its amphitheatre of Riesling vineyards – the town is pretty too, but here the striking surroundings that yield equally stunning wines are what really count.*

SAARBURG

RECOMMENDED PRODUCERS

Weingut Forstmeister Geltz Zilliken
Heckingstrasse 20
D 54439 Saarburg
Tel: (06581) 2456
Hanno Zilliken's wines from Saarburg and Ockfen are steely and minerally with great ageing potential. Stop here for sensational Auslesen/BA/Eisweins. By appointment only.

Weingut Dr Heinz Wagner
Bahnhofstrasse 3
D 54439 Saarburg
Tel: (06581) 2457
Produces classic Saar Rieslings. Even winemaker Heinz Wagner's simplest wines are clean, racy and full of fruit. By appointment only.

Hausen-Mabilon
Im Staden 114–124
D 54439 Saarburg
Tel: (05681) 3044
Dependable producer of quality Sekt, both Riesling and Elbling.

HOTELS

Weinhaus Ayler Kupp
See restaurants.

Zunftstube
Am Markt 11
D 54439 Saarburg
Tel: (06581) 3696
Pleasant, moderately priced hotel.

RESTAURANTS

Weinhaus Ayler Kupp
Trierer Strasse 49
D 54441 Ayl
Tel: (06581) 3031
Julia Lauer's excellent country cooking, good wines from the Lauer estate, and stylish and modern hotel rooms are all good reasons to stop here. Moderate prices, too.

Burg-Restaurant
Auf dem Burgberg
D 54439
Tel: (06581) 2622
Fine restaurant in Saarburg's castle. Fish dishes are particularly good, and the list of Saar wines is impressive.

PLACES OF INTEREST

Glockengieserei Mabilon
Saarburg's famous bell foundry can be visited during working hours.

Kastel-Staadt Klause
The architect Schinkel constructed this beautiful chapel high above the Saar for Prussian King Friedrich Wilhelm IV in 1838. The last part of the climb is by foot (Tuesday–Saturday 9am–noon and 1–4.30pm).

Rausch (meaning 'roar') of the Leukbach waterfall situated in the centre of Saarburg's *Altstadt*. The Altstadt is dominated by the medieval *Burg*, or fortified tower, that stands on a rocky headland by the river, and the town takes its name from both the Saar and the Burg.

With two leading wine estates and a *Sekt* (sparkling wine) company, Saarburg offers more than sightseeing. The special minerally intensity of the Rausch wines is no less of a reason to call here than the beautifully restored Baroque and Renaissance architecture of the *Oberstadt* (Upper Town).

Cross over the river using the B407 to reach the suburb of Beurig. Watch carefully for the turning to Schloss Saarstein because the sign is small. Take this turning and the road climbs through an ancient forest to reach the castle's commanding hilltop position with a spectacular view. Beware, though: in the winter this is the place to experience the cold winds that give Saar Rieslings their characteristic steely acidity. The wines of Serrig are almost always marked by this steeliness, even in the best vintages. In summer, however, you can bask on the sunlit terrace here and enjoy the refined richness of classic Saar wines.

SERRIG

The view from the Bert Simon estate on the southern side of Serrig, where a great part of the Saar's course can be seen, is no less impressive than Schloss Saarstein's. Bert Simon's Herrenberg and Würtzberg vineyards lie just off the bottom edge of the Saar map. Here the vineyards end, but the magnificent scenery continues south (most famously with the great Saar loop close to Mettlach). Return to Beurig and ask for the Saarburg railway station. The Dr Wagner estate is just a few doors away in one of the Saarburg's most imposing houses; built from sparkling wine profits when Saar Sekt was more expensive than champagne. Take the small road signposted Wiltingen.

OCKFEN

Two kilometres downstream and a sharp right turn under the railway line brings you to Ockfen and its famous Bockstein vineyard. The village of Ockfen nestling within this great amphitheatre of vines is a sight that inclines one to disagree with Jancis Robinson's assertion that vineyards are no more interesting to look at than potato fields. The village itself is not more attractive than many in the area, save for its graceful church spire, but the town's renown as a source of fine Riesling more than makes up for whatever it may lack on the architectural front. Dr Fischer's is the only well-known estate based here, although Dr Wagner and Zilliken also make fine Ockfen wines. At their best, Bockstein Rieslings are more perfumed than other Saar wines, combining succulence with raciness.

SERRIG AND OCKFEN

RECOMMENDED PRODUCERS

Weingut Schloss Saarstein
D 54455 Serrig
Tel: (06581) 232
Christian Ebert's wines combine the steeliness typical of Saar wines with vibrant fruit. A high general standard; great Eiswein. By appointment only.

Weingut Bert Simon
Herrenberg
D 54455 Serrig
Tel: (06581) 2208
Erratic producer whose best Spätlesen/Auslesen can be excellent. Makes good, dry Weissburgunder. By appointment only.

Weingut Dr Heinz Wagner
See Saarburg.

Weingut Forstmeister Geltz Zilliken
See Saarburg.

Left *Great treasures are found in these old barrels at Saarburg's Weingut Zilliken: the Beerenauslesen and Eiswein are some of the region's most stunning.*
Below *Spring at Schloss Saarstein: time for the vines to recover from the icy winter winds which sweep down the Saar Valley to give the wines their distinctive steeliness.*

Northern Saar

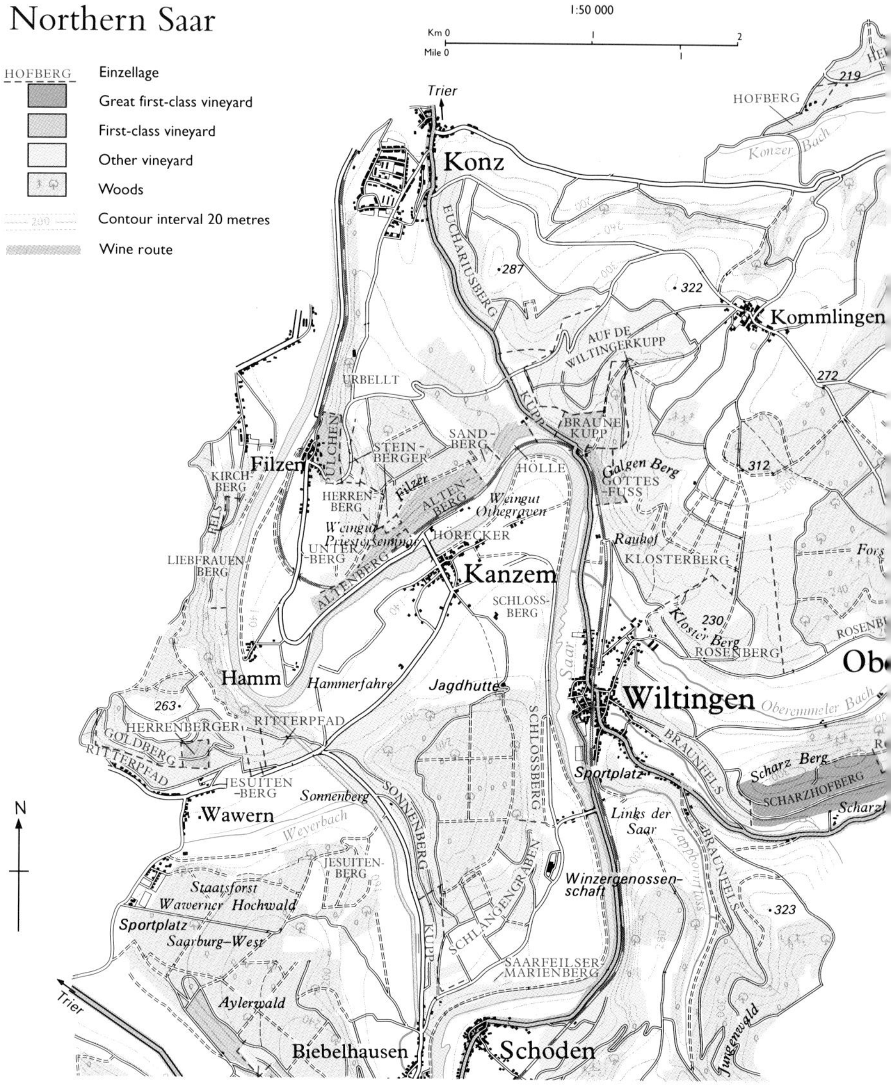

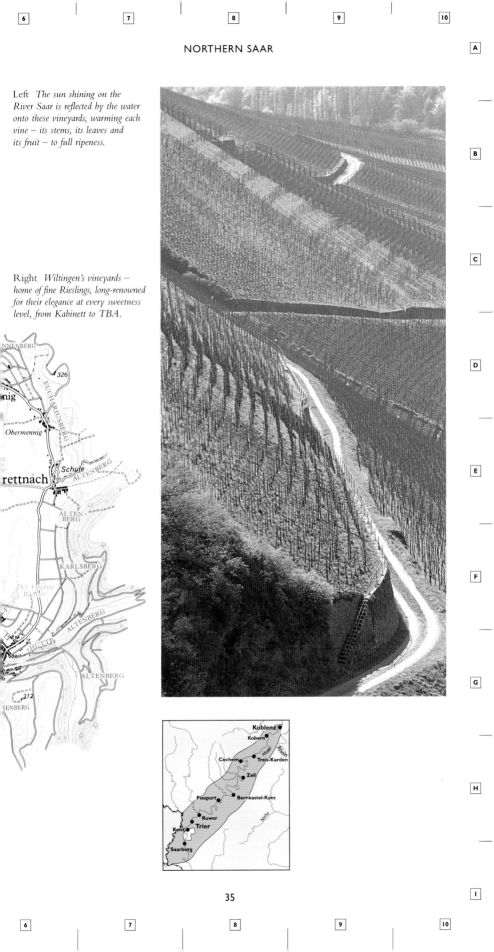

Left *The sun shining on the River Saar is reflected by the water onto these vineyards, warming each vine – its stems, its leaves and its fruit – to full ripeness.*

Right *Wiltingen's vineyards – home of fine Rieslings, long-renowned for their elegance at every sweetness level, from Kabinett to TBA.*

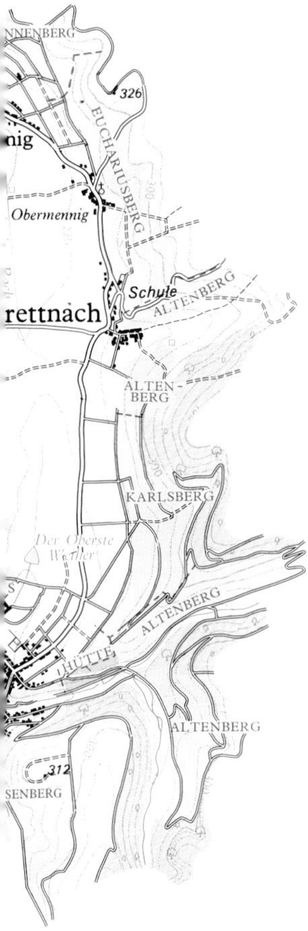

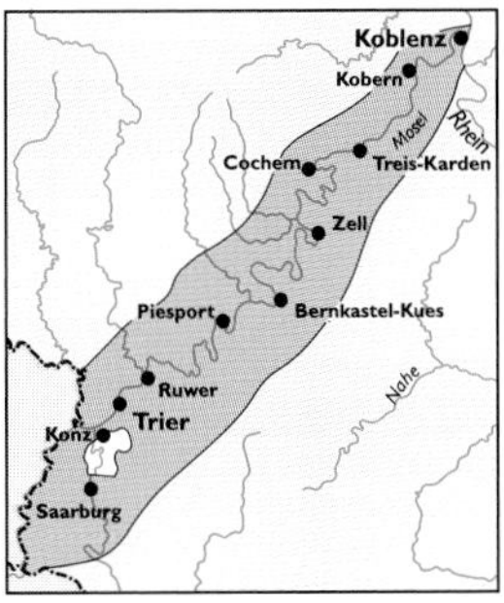

Above *The imposing doorway of Weingut Egon Müller in Scharzhof – as imposing as the wines behind it.*

Right *Wiltingen has vineyards of every gradient: the steepest ones, with the best aspect of all, are those of the soaring Scharzhofberg.*

WILTINGEN

After returning to the river road, turn right towards the village of Wiltingen, where imposing 19th-century houses reveal how much money was once made here from winemaking. However fine the wines from Wiltingen's other vineyards may be, those made from the grapes of the world-famous Scharzhofberg have given the village its reputation. To reach it, just ask the locals for directions to Oberemmel.

After crossing the railway line, the road climbs steeply out of Wiltingen along a narrow valley; the precipitous slopes of the Scharzhofberg soar into the sky on the left. Here are the vines that add all the extra dimenions to Wiltingen wines. The Auslesen, for example, possess an elegant honey-and-dried fruit character; they are said to be the richest in the entire region, and are ranked among the world's finest dessert wines. At the foot of this vineyard lies the 18th-century Scharzhof, home of the famous Egon Müller estate where these excellent dessert wines are made.

WILTINGEN

RECOMMENDED PRODUCERS

Weingut Egon Müller-Scharzhof
Scharzhof
D 54459 Wiltingen
Tel: (06501) 17232
One of Germany's great estates with Rieslings of classical elegance. Everything from Auslese upwards is of world-class quality and correspondingly priced. Strictly by appointment only, and no sales to visitors.

Weingut Jordan und Jordan
Dehenstrasse 2
D 54459 Wiltingen
Tel: (06501) 16510
Love them or loathe them, Peter Jordan's uncompromising dry wines are unique Saar Rieslings. Appointment recommended; closed Sunday.

Weingut von Hövel
Agritiusstrasse 56
D 54329 Oberemmel
Tel: (06501) 15384
Eberhard von Kunow makes the richest, most succulent wines on the Saar. The Kabinetts and Spätlesen are excellent quality and offer good value for money. By appointment only.

Weingut Johann Peter Reinert
Alter Weg 7a
D 54441 Kanzem
Tel: (06501) 13277
This little-known, small estate makes very clean, fruity wines, all extremely good value. By appointment only.

The road continues to the wine village of Oberemmel, ringed by vine-clothed hills. The Rieslings here, particularly those from the Agritiusberg, Raul and the first-class Hütte sites, are an ideal introduction to Saar wines because they often possess a marvellous fruity charm and are not too severe. The Reichsgraf von Kesselstatt and von Hövel estates are fine examples of what Oberemmel is capable of producing. Von Hövel is situated just a few yards from the village church.

Drive back to Wiltingen and turn back on to the river road. From here, there is a splendid view across the Saar to the Altenberg vineyard of Kanzem. See how this great slope catches the sun and is perfectly sheltered by the surrounding hills. It is easy to believe local vintners who maintain that it is second only to the great Scharzhofberg.

The road then climbs steeply through the Wiltinger Braune Kupp vineyard, where you should look back over the Saar. Konz and Trier are only a short drive away.

Weingut von Othegraven
Weinstrasse 1
D 54441 Kanzem
Tel: (06501) 150042
Recently Frau Dr Kegel has put this estate back on course to rejoin the Saar elite. Appointment recommended; closed Sunday.

Weingut Piedmont
Saartal 1
D 54329 Filzen
Tel: (06501) 99009
Claus and Monika Piedmont concentrate on producing light, fresh, dry and off-dry Rieslings. Appointment recommended; closed Sunday.

THE RUWER VALLEY

Although Ruwer wines are often spoken of in the same breath as those of the Saar, they are as distinct as these valleys' landscapes. The Ruwer Valley is narrower and more sheltered than that of the Saar, and thus climatically less severe. Its natural charm has made it a desirable part of Trier's commuter belt, but new buildings have been discreetly tucked away. There are little more than 250 hectares of vineyards here, compared to five times this area on the Saar. However, two world-famous estates and several other fine producers have given its vivacious, aromatic wines a good name.

To reach the Ruwer Valley, take the A602 *Autobahn* north out of Trier, leaving by the Kenn/Ruwer exit. Follow the signs for Ruwer until you reach the village, where you turn left towards Eitelsbach. The idyllic Karthäuserhof estate is reached by a small, tree-lined private road from the centre of the village (immediately before the junction, the estate's vineyards appear on the left; look for the impossibly small sign, or ask). Stand in the courtyard here when the clock in the medieval tower chimes the hour, and it is hard to believe that the Carthusian monks, who tended these vineyards between 1335 until secularization in 1803, are not still busy among the vines and cellars.

The other great estate, Maximin Grünhaus, is less than one kilometre away on the other side of the valley. Take the small road from Eitelsbach to Mertesdorf past Hotel Weiss and turn right there to reach the main road running along the valley. Grünhaus is on the right-hand side, unmissable with its Gothic-style buildings, battlements and the magnificent trees in its grounds – a fairy-tale German castle. Much of what can be seen today is not as old as it looks, because the estate was remodelled

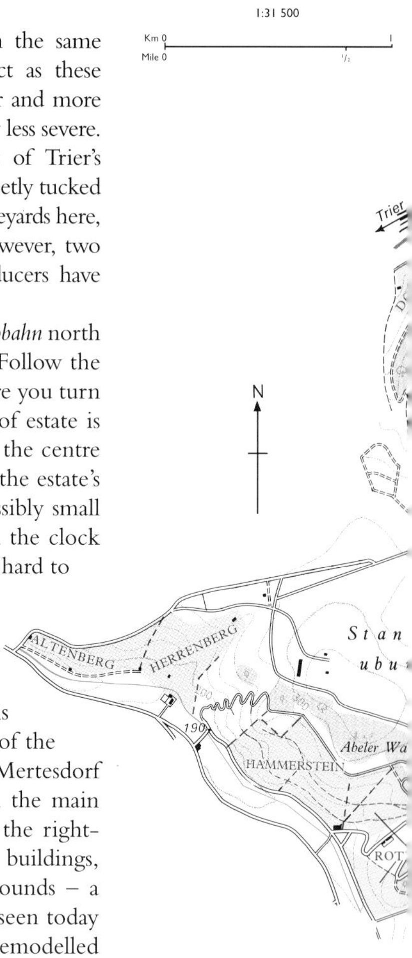

Above *Although an increasingly popular place to live, the valley of the Ruwer retains its charm, its old buildings remain uncluttered by new.* Right *Weingut Maximin Grünhaus: its buildings have an unmistakable, unmissable style – apt frontage for equally distinctive wines.*

THE RUWER VALLEY

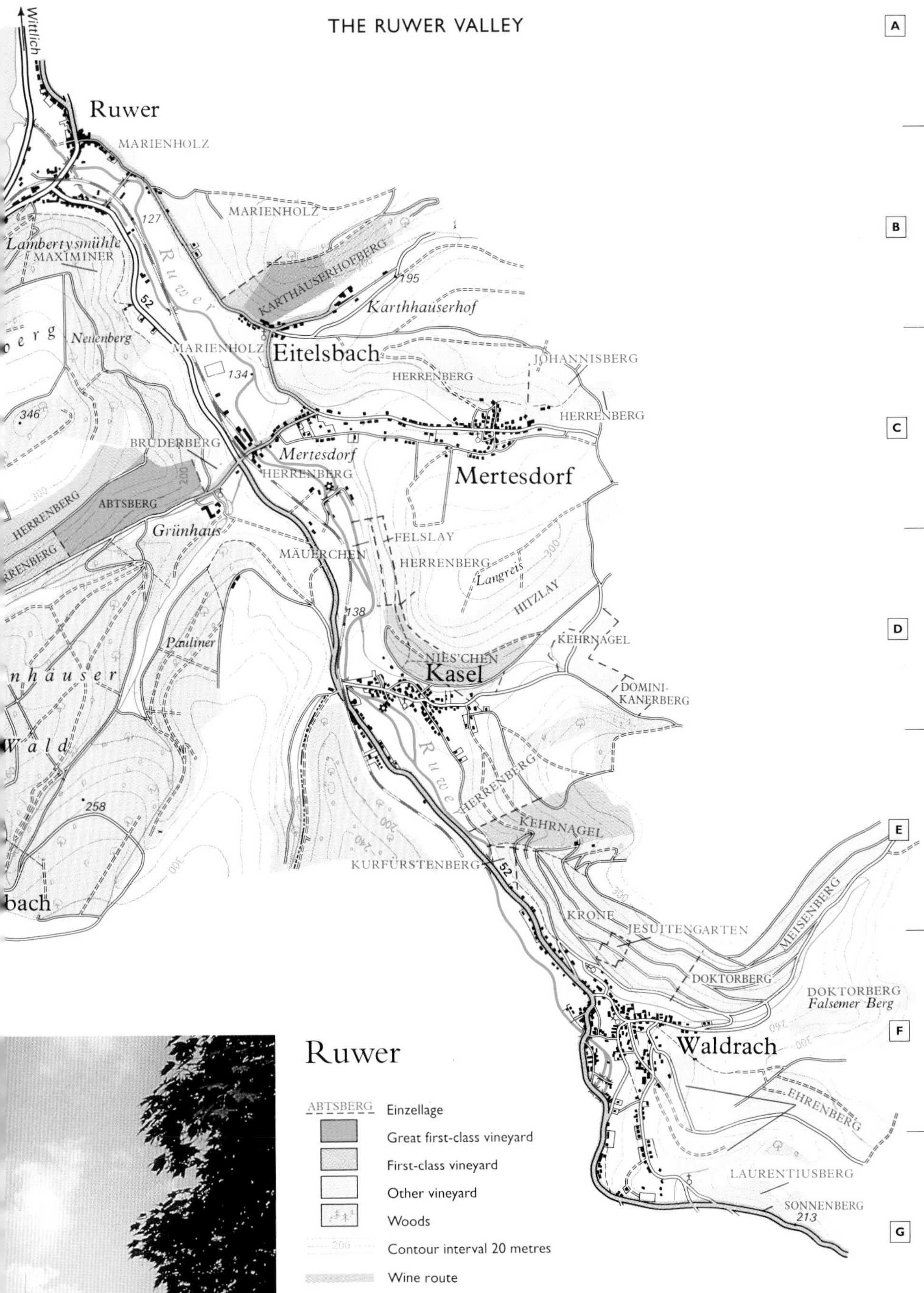

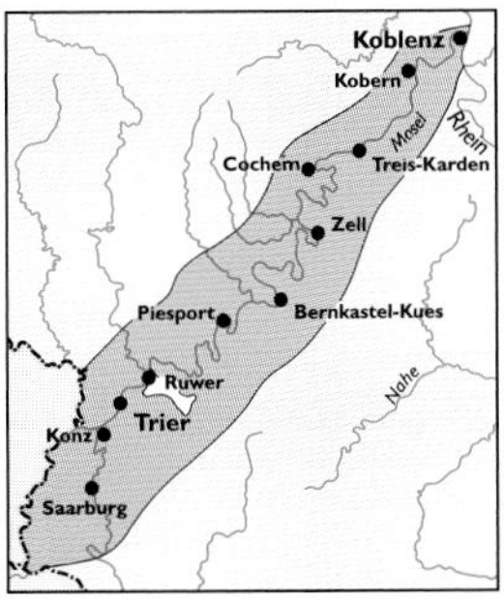

The grounds of the great Maximin Grünhaus estate (right) are not solely devoted to vines, for there are many beautiful trees too. The history lies with the vineyards, however – some date back to 966AD.

in 1882 by the von Schubert family. However, the recorded history of these vineyards goes back over a thousand years to 966AD, and the oldest part of the cellars appears to be Roman. Unusually for Germany, both Grünhaus and Karthäuserhof have their vineyards close to the estate buildings, much like a Bordeaux château. The Grünhaus vineyards covering the whole of the south-facing slope are particularly beautiful, though the roads through them are, sadly, private.

From here, continue along the main road to Kasel and Waldrach. On your left is the hotel and wine estate of Karlsmühle. It stands on the site of a Roman mill where imported Italian marble was cut for the grand buildings of Trier; the Roman poet Ausonius mentions it in his poem *Mosella* of 371AD. This idyllic corner is definitely worth a stop, as much for the scenery as for its wines.

Follow the main road another kilometre to the charming village of Kasel. It owes its fame to the Rieslings from the first-class Nies'chen and Kehrnagel vineyards. Next door lie the Lorenzhöfer vineyards (Felslay and Mäuerchen) of Karlsmühle. All yield classic Ruwer Rieslings, aromatic and expressive.

THE RUWER VALLEY

RECOMMENDED PRODUCERS

C von Schubert'che Gutsverwaltung Maximin Grünhaus
D 54318 Mertesdorf
Tel: (0651) 5111
Dr Carl von Schubert's Rieslings are famous the world over for their aromatic complexity and racy elegance. All the wines are of excellent quality, from dry QbA up to noble Auslesen. Strictly by appointment; closed Saturday afternoon and Sunday.

Weingut Karlsmühle
Im Mühlengrund 1
D 54318 Mertesdorf
Tel: (0651) 5123
Peter Geiben can be chaotic, but he makes some of the most expressive, aromatic Ruwer Rieslings – very good value. By appointment only. The Karlsmühle hotel and restaurant are rustic, but their situation idyllic.

Gutsverwaltung Rautenstrauch'sche Karthäuserhof
D 54292 Eitelsbach
Tel: (0651) 5121
Extremely vivid and steely, Christoph Tyrell's dry wines may be too severe for some. However, those with natural sweetness are of dazzling brilliance. By appointment only; closed at weekends.

Weingut von Beulwitz
Hauptstrasse 1
D-54318 Kasel
Tel: (0651) 5134
Greatly improved quality in recent years. Elegant wines from Kanzem's top vineyards. By appointment only.

Winzergenossenschaft Kasel
Schulstrasse 1
54317 Kasel
Tel: (0651) 52117
Germany's smallest cooperative of four hectares is a dependable source for fruity Kasel Rieslings. By appointment only.

HOTELS

Hotel Weiss
Eitelsbacher Strasse 4
D 54318 Mertesdorf
Tel: (0651) 5134
Comfortable, modern hotel with fine views. Herr Weiss also owns the von Beulwitz estate of Kasel.

RESTAURANTS

Restaurant Grünhäuser Mühle
Hauptstrasse 4
D 54318 Mertesdorf
Tel: (0651) 52434
Pleasant country cooking, moderately priced.

Maximin Grünhaus and Karthäuserhof are the two great estates of the Ruwer Valley. Karthäuserhof (below) *is tricky to find, but when you do, you may find yourself transported back in time by relics of its monastic past.*

From Lorenzhöfer, drive on to Waldrach. There may no important wine estates here, but this is perhaps the most picturesque part of the entire valley. Vine-clad, south-facing slopes and the densely forested, less favoured hillsides almost enclose the village. Few tourists make it up here, and the hustle and bustle of Trier seems a world away.

Waldrach always needs a hot summer for its wines to shine, but when they are good, they have the freshness and floral charm that makes even the lesser Ruwer wines hard to resist. From here, it is possible to climb further, but the vineyards begin to thin out as you get closer to the cold winds of the Hunsrück hills. The return journey to Trier takes about half an hour.

The Middle Mosel

The narrow, winding Mosel Valley is one of the most imposing and remarkable wine landscapes in the world. William Turner's recently rediscovered watercolours of the region, painted in 1839, depict as much. Nowhere are there more precipitous vineyards than those clinging to these valley sides; nowhere are vineyard soils more stony and inhospitable. However, it is equally true that no other wine-growing region looks more verdant than the Mosel Valley in the summer months, the result of the regions relatively high rainfall. This combination of harshness and luxuriance results in some of the most expressive, aromatic and elegant white wines in the world.

The Middle Mosel is the most famous section of this valley, and one of the most important producers of high-quality Riesling wines in all of Germany. For purists, it extends from Trittenheim to Erden and not a kilometre further in either direction. The most generous definition of the region takes it from Schweich, just downstream from Trier where the Mosel enters the narrow section of its valley, right the way to Zell, which is halfway between Trier and Koblenz. Either way, it is one of the most exciting winemaking areas in Germany.

Less well-known than the Middle Mosel itself are the tributary valleys which radiate from it, and the hill country of the Eifel and the Hunsrück. While fine weather is needed to explore them properly, they are certainly worth the effort, and offer fascinating contrasts to the Mosel itself. The rocky crags of the Veldenz Valley, the dense forests of the Hunsrück, with the remains of pre-Roman settlements, and the volcanic lakes of the Eifel hills are facets of the region which any visitor who is not intent on packing every day full of tastings should not miss.

Left *Few of Germany's vineyards are lusher than those of the Mosel Valley in the summer – conditions are ideal for vines, which consequently thrive in every available corner. Piesport* (above) *is home to some of the finest.*

LEIWEN AND TRITTENHEIM

Although some good wines are made further upstream, the first concentration of important producers is to be found at Leiwen. Try to find time to take the scenic route here from Trier – the B53 along the Mosel Valley. Leave the B53 shortly before Klüserrath, taking the bridge to Thörnich, then follow the signs for Leiwen. Once a centre for the mass production of cheap wines from inferior modern grapes, Leiwen has recently undergone an astonishing transformation thanks to the efforts of a new generation of winemakers – a glowing example of the recent Mosel wine renaissance. There are now a handful of interesting estates based in Leiwen's otherwise unremarkable streets. In recent years, they have begun to discover what rich, subtle wines the steep slopes of the Leiwener Laurentiuslay (on the opposite bank of the Mosel) can produce. Carl Loewen currently leads the pack.

In Leiwen, ask for directions to Summit, the town's exclusive suburb perched high up in the valley. From the terrace of the Hotel Summit there is a breathtaking panoramic view over two of the Mosel's great loops, and downstream almost as far as Piesport. This spot has some

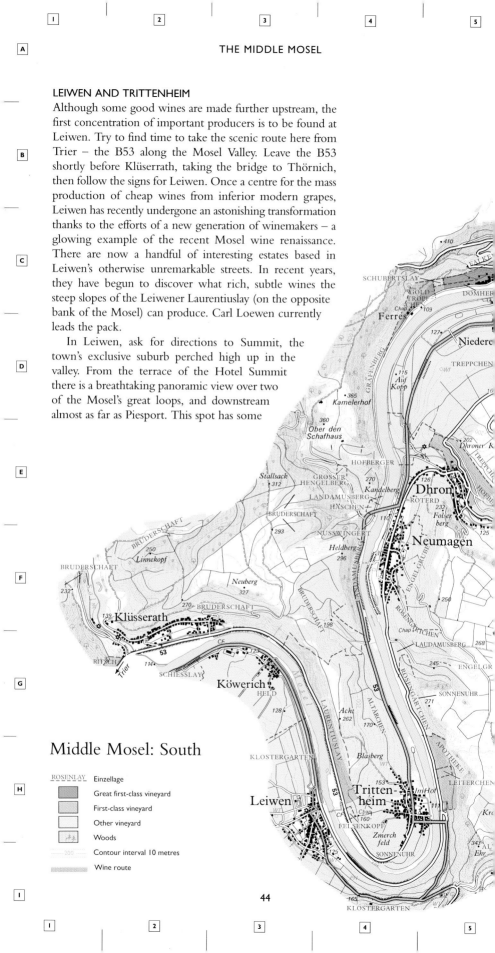

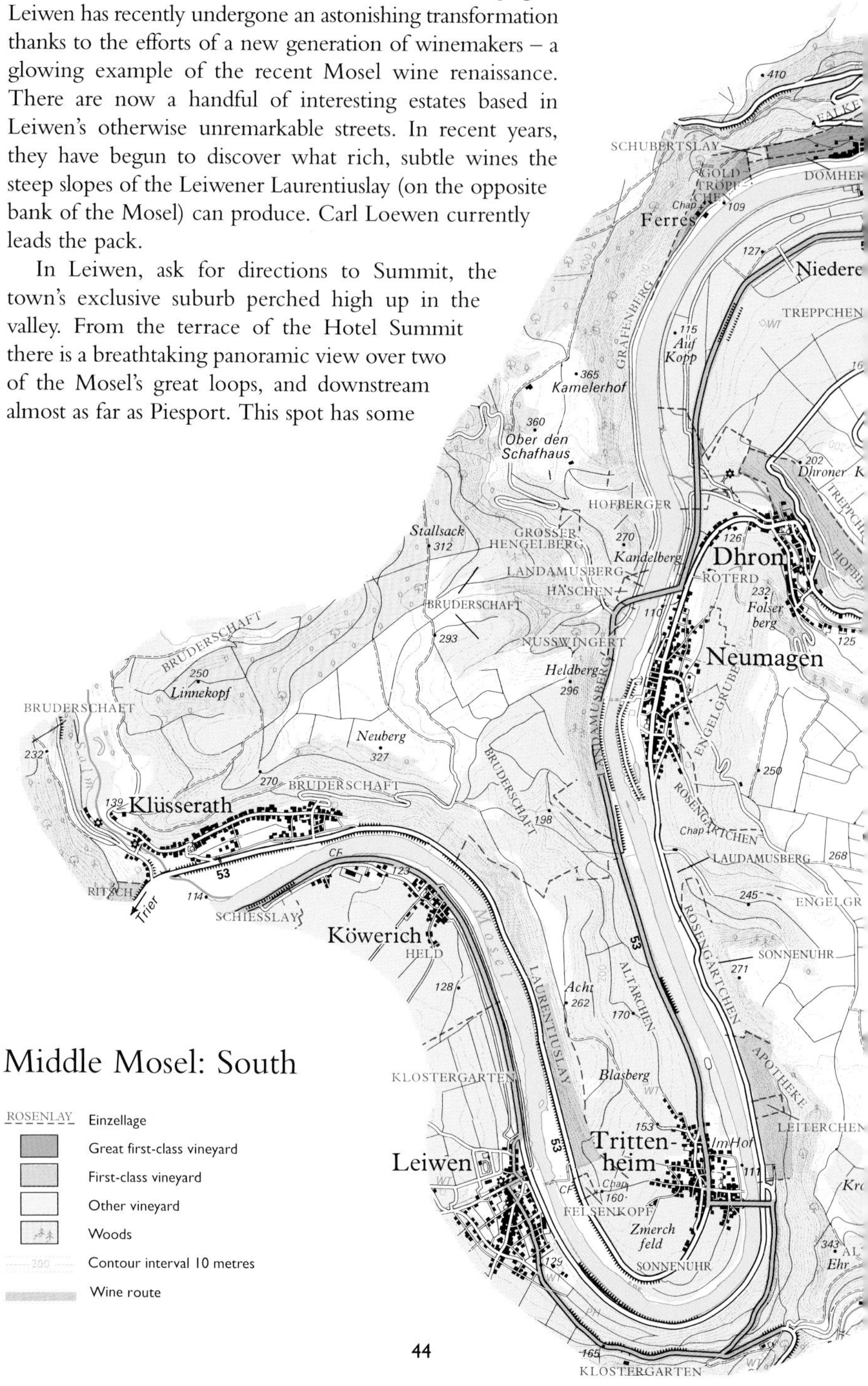

Middle Mosel: South

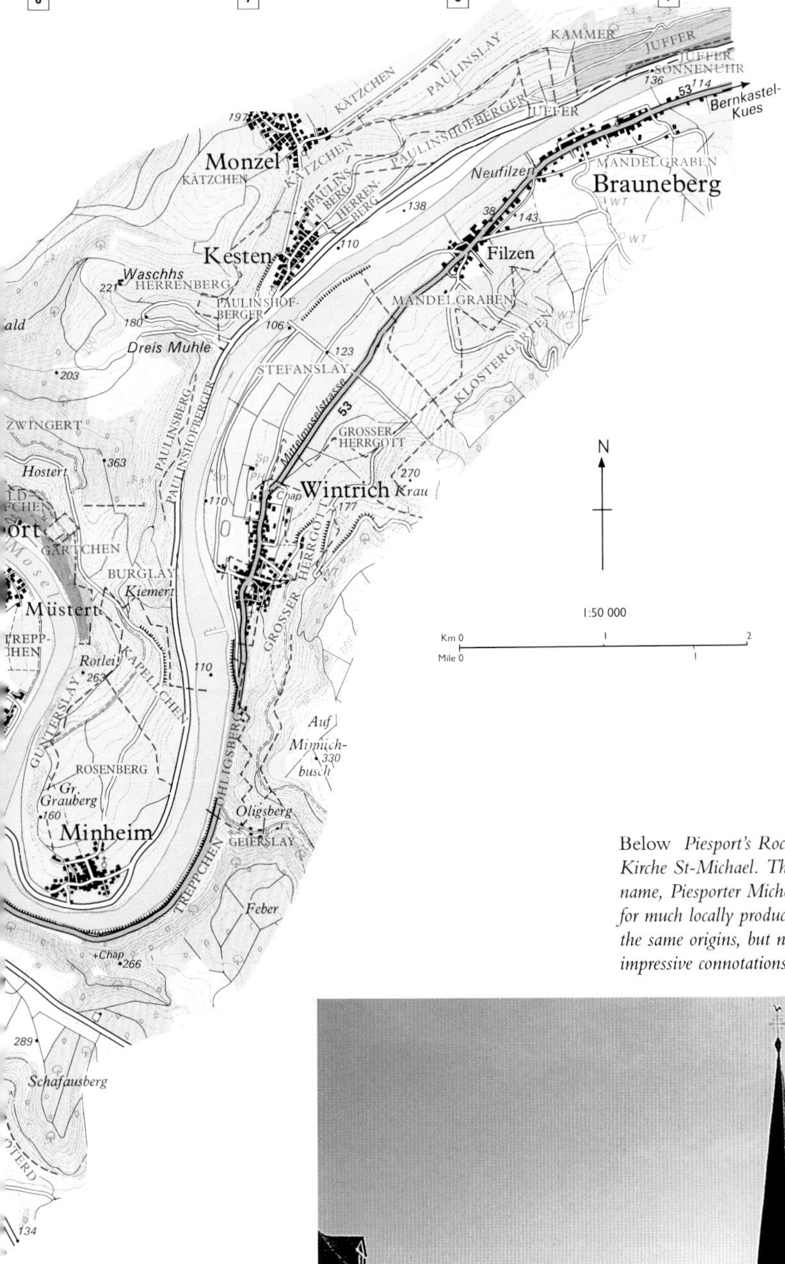

Below *Piesport's Rococo church: Kirche St-Michael. The Grosslage name, Piesporter Michelsberg, used for much locally produced wine, has the same origins, but not such impressive connotations.*

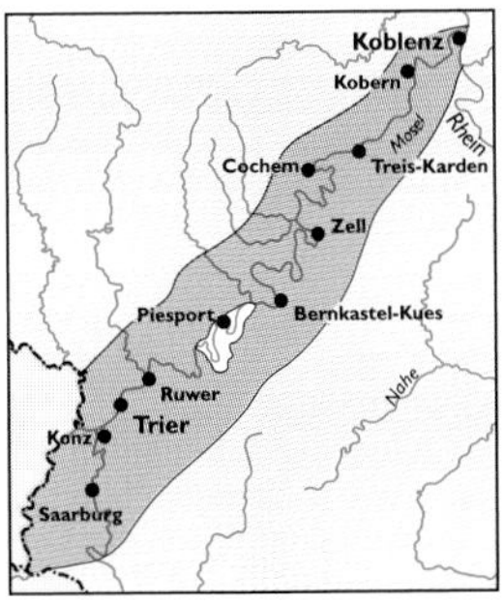

LEIWEN AND TRITTENHEIM

RECOMMENDED PRODUCERS

Weingut Carl Loewen
Matthiasstrasse 30, D 54340 Leiwen
Tel: (06507) 3094
Winemaker Karl Loewen makes good wines from little-known Pöllich and Detzem, and fine Spätlesen/Auslesen from the Leiwener Laurentiuslay. By appointment only; closed Sunday.

Weingut Sankt Urbanshof
D 54340 Leiwen
Tel: (06507) 3041
Large estate owned by Hermann Weiss making very clean, mainly dry wines. Appointment recommended; open weekends.

Weingut Grans-Fassian
Römerstrasse 28, D 54340 Leiwen
Tel: (06507) 3170
Rather erratic, but when on form Gerhard Grans hits the bull's-eye with his intense Rieslings from Trittenheim's top sites. By appointment only.

Weingut Ernst Clüsserath
Moselweinstrasse 67
D 54349 Trittenheim
Tel: (06507) 2607
Rich wines with plenty of character. By appointment only.

Weingut Milz-Laurentiushof
Moselstrasse 7–9, D 54349 Trittenheim
Tel: (06507) 2300
Traditional-style wines that do not always live up to the estate's high reputation. By appointment only; closed weekends.

Weingut Clüsserath-Weiler
Haus an der Brücke
D 54349 Trittenheim
Tel: (06507) 5011
Wines with plenty of body, but some lack elegance. By appointment only.

HOTEL/RESTAURANT

Gutshotel von Kesselstatt
Balduistrasse 1
D 54347 Neumagen-Dhron
Tel: (06507) 2035
The most comfortable hotel in this part of the Mosel. Dieter Braun's cooking can be very good.

RESTAURANTS

Laurentiusstuben
Moselweinstr 8, D 54349 Trittenheim
Tel: (06507) 2209
Dependable restaurant with short menu of well-prepared dishes.

Restaurant zur Malerklause
Im Hofecken
D 54413 Bescheid
Tel: (06509) 558
High up in the Hünsruck, 8km from Trittenheim. Tasty, unpretentious meals with a long list of Mosel wines.

almost impossibly romantic sunsets. Drive back down to the Mosel, crossing the bridge to Trittenheim. The recent success of Leiwen has stimulated the winemakers of Trittenheim to commit themselves more seriously to quality wine production, and there are now three significant producers here. Directly opposite the village are the excellent Apotheke and Leiterchen vineyards (the latter a monopoly of the Milz estate). Their wines are sleek and minerally, the best possessing a classical elegance.

Rejoin the B53 in Trittenheim, turning right in the direction of Neumagen-Dhron. The wines of this twin town have always stood in the shadows of those from both Trittenheim and Piesport, although in a good vintage those from the Dhroner Hofberg are juicy and substantial. Neumagen was founded in the third century AD as a Roman fort, and is best known for the sculpture of a Roman wine ship which was excavated here. The wine barrels in the ship look strikingly similar to the 1,000-litre *Fuder* casks used in winemaking in the region today. Continue on to Piesport, where even more remarkable Roman remains have been recently discovered.

PIESPORT

No other community's name stands for both the most glorious and depressing side winemaking in the Mosel than that of Piesport. Vast quantities of inferior wine are sold under the Grosslage name Piesporter Michelsberg, most of which is neither Riesling nor from the vineyards of

Piesport. It is a sad but unavoidable fact that these products legally exploit the reputation of the superb Rieslings that are produced from the great first-class Goldtröpfchen and Domherr vineyard sites of Piesport. The latter can be beautifully majestic wines, with an almost Baroque richness of fruit and aroma, yet with a firm structure and a long life expectancy.

At the centre of the great amphitheatre of vines which makes up the top sites of Piesport (at the western extremity of the village) lie the remains of a Roman pressing house. One of the presses has been reconstructed, and each year, during the first weekend in October, local vintners recreate Roman-style wine pressing. Drive up to the forest which crowns Piesport's vineyards and you will see almost the same view that Ausonius described in his *Mosella*. The village of Piesport has hardly changed during recent decades, and is still dominated by impressive 17th- and 18th-century houses and the Rococo church of Saint Michael (1776–77). Here there are a clutch of fine producers, including Reinhold Haart, who makes some of the finest wines in the region.

PIESPORT

RECOMMENDED PRODUCERS

Weingut Reinhold Haart
Ausoniusufer 18
D 54498 Piesport
Tel: (06507) 2015
Theo Haart's rich, explosively fruity Rieslings from Piesport and Wintrich belong to the first rank of German wines. Few, but excellent, dry wines. By appointment only; closed Sunday.

Weingut Reuscher-Haart
Sankt-Michael-Strasse 20–22
D 54498 Piesport
Tel: (06507) 2492
The traditional Piesport wines from Hugo Schwang are never short of power or character. By appointment only.

Weingut Kurt Hain
Am Domhof 5
D 54498 Piesport
Tel: (06507) 6879
Young Gernot Hain makes elegant, complex Piesport Rieslings. The wines can be tasted at the family's hotel and restaurant, Piesporter Goldtröpfchen.

Weingut Weller-Lehnert
St Michel Strasse 27–29
D 54498 Piesport
Tel: (06507) 2498
One of the most dependable sources for real Piesport wines. Substantial Rieslings with plenty of fruit. By appointment only.

Juice from pressed grapes – red or white – was once collected in vessels such as this one in Piesport (above). Left *Trittenheim's vineyards are extensive and, as ever, beautifully tended, but only recently has their potential begun to be realized.*

BRAUNEBERG

RECOMMENDED PRODUCERS

Weingut Fritz Haag
Dusemonder Strasse 44
D 54472 Brauneberg
Tel: (06534) 410
One of the Mosel's most famous names. Fruit purity and racy elegance are the hallmarks of Wilhelm Haag's highly sought-after Brauneberg Rieslings. Strictly by appointment only.

Weingut Willi Haag
Hauptstrasse 111
D 54472 Brauneberg
Tel: (06534) 450
Marcus Haag's full-bodied, lush Spätlesen and Auslesen from Brauneberg's top sites offer very good value. By appointment only.

Weingut Karp-Schreiber
Hauptstrasse 118
D 54472 Brauneberg
Tel: (06534) 236
Alwin Karp's small estate makes some of the most powerful wines from the Brauneberg. By appointment only.

Weingut Bastgen
Moselstrasse 1
D 54518 Kesten
Tel: (06535) 7142
Armin Vogel and Mona Bastgen have rapidly made a name for expressive, well-made Rieslings. By appointment only.

Weingut Schloss Lieser
Am Markt 1
D 54470 Lieser
Tel: (06531) 6431
Recently Thomas Haag (son of Wilhelm) has put this estate back on the map with rich, polished wines. By appointment only.

Weingut Max Ferd Richter
Hauptstrasse 85
D 54486 Mülheim
Tel: (06534) 704
Dirk Richter makes a wide range of consistently impressive wines from vineyards scattered between Brauneberg and Traben-Trarbach. Excellent Eiswein. Appointment recommended; closed Sunday.

HOTELS

Brauneberger Hof
Hauptstrasse 66
D 54472 Brauneberg
Tel: (06534) 1400
A beautiful 18th-century half-timbered hotel with a modern extension. Very comfortable rooms and a good restaurant. Moderate prices and good value. Sadly, unexciting wines.

Hotel Richtershof
See restaurants.

BRAUNEBERG

Cross back over the Mosel to rejoin the B53 and drive on to Brauneberg. Until the middle of this century, no Mosel wines enjoyed higher international standing than Rieslings from the Brauneberg; at their best, they are big and intense, yet very polished. Over the last 20 years the Fritz Haag estate has catapulted Brauneberg back to the top again. Although the village's main street is lined with substantial stone-built houses, the scantness of half-timbering and gables here gives it an austerity quite distinct from that of its neighbours. The great wall of slate and vines that is the Brauneberg looms over the village which takes its name. Today it is divided into the Juffer, Juffer-Sonnenuhr and Kammer sites. The Haags are the leading winemakers here; confusingly, Wilhelm Haag runs the Fritz Haag estate, while Inge and Marcus Haag run the Willi Haag estate. Willi Haag is in the middle of the village, Fritz Haag in the back streets.

After passing though Brauneberg, the B53 bypasses the attractive wine village of Mülheim. Turn off here to visit the important Max Ferd Richter estate, and the hotel

Hotel Mehn zum Niederburg
Moselstrasse 2
D 54470 Lieser
Tel: (06531) 9570
Comfortable, moderately-priced hotel near the river. The restaurant offers simple but solid food.

RESTAURANTS

Restaurant Elisenberg/ Hotel Richtershof
(in Gutshotel Richtershof)
Hauptstrasse 81
D 54486 Mülheim
Tel: (06534) 93730
Newly opened complex in beautiful old buildings. Hotel is medium-sized, very comfortable; restaurant is sophisticated, with international, almost Michelin-standard, cuisine; both quite expensive. Director, well-known wine waiter Markus del Monego, has high ambitions for the Elisenberg.

Restaurant zur Post
Hauptstrasse 65
D 54486 Mülheim
Tel: (06534) 1321
An unpretentious restaurant with good home cooking that has a lighter touch than usually found in the region.

PLACES OF INTEREST

Veldenz
Reached from Mülheim, Veldenz is one of the most beautiful villages in the Mosel region. Above it stand the remains of Burg Veldenz. The town's wines deserve to be better known.

and restaurant, Richtershof, both built during the Mosel's Golden Era at the end of the 19th century. Take the bridge cross the river from Mülheim to Lieser. From the bridge there are magnificent views of the Brauneberg, and of the huge, grey slate bulk of Schloss Lieser, a castle that was built at the end of the 19th century and is now a modern business school. Not surprisingly for this area, the eponymous wine estate is under the guidance of yet another member of the Haag family: this time, Thomas, son of Wilhelm, who is predicted to be as successful as his father. If his first two vintages are anything to go by, then Schloss Lieser will soon be in the first rank of Middle Mosel producers.

Top *Schloss Lieser: an imposing building whose attached wine estate is one of the region's leaders.*
Above *Brauneberg's vineyards are divided into three highly esteemed sites: this one is Brauneberger Juffer.*

THE MIDDLE MOSEL

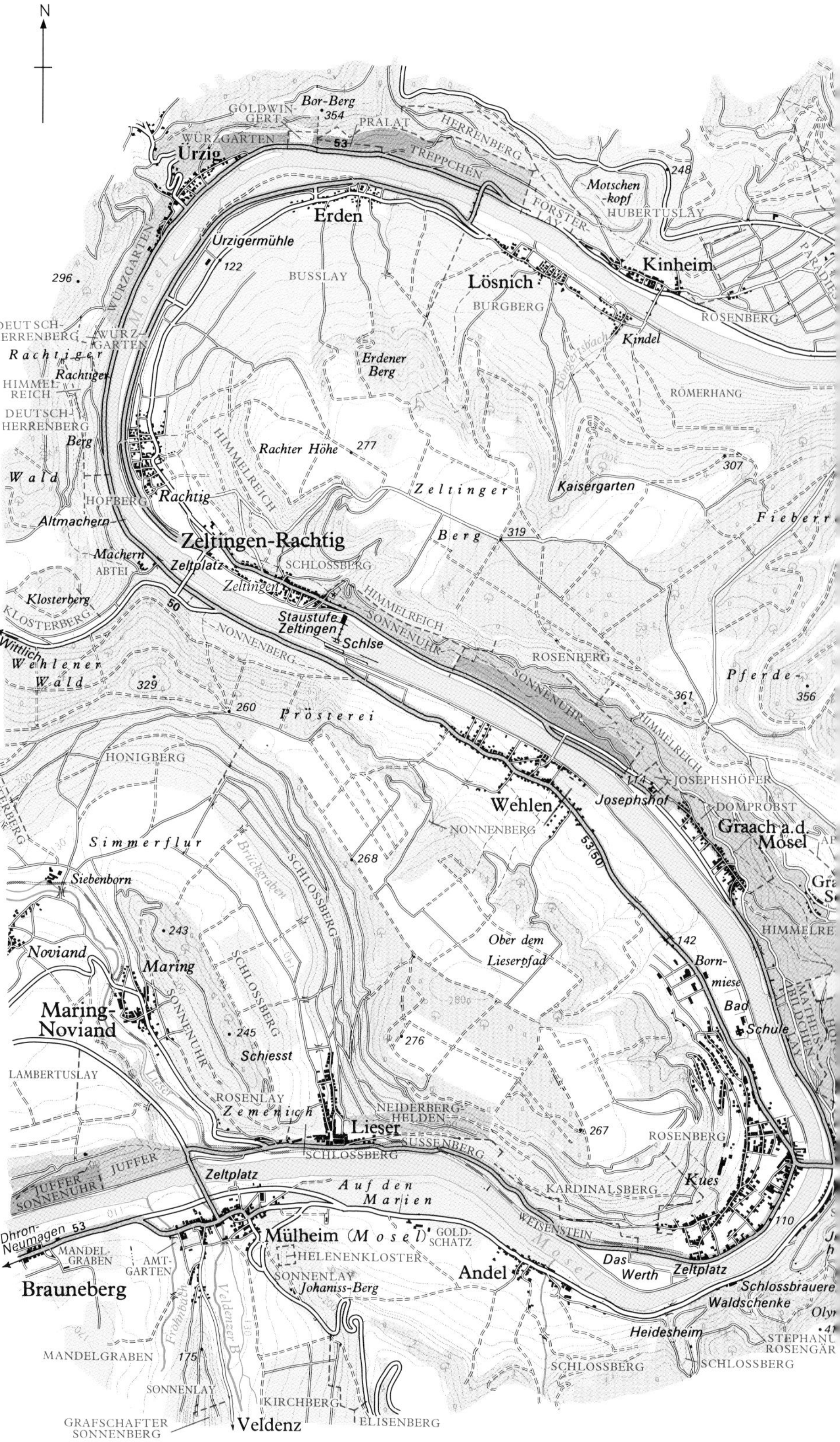

Middle Mosel: North

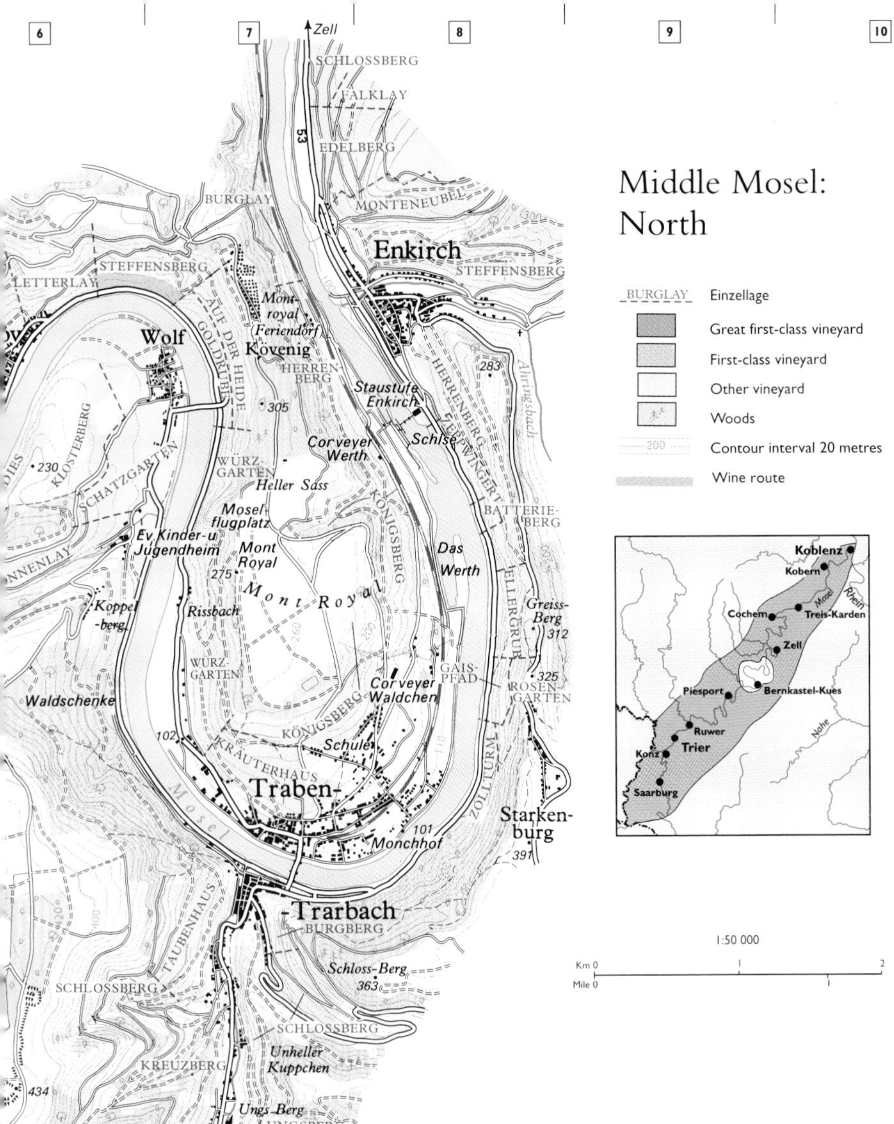

BERNKASTEL-KUES AND GRAACH

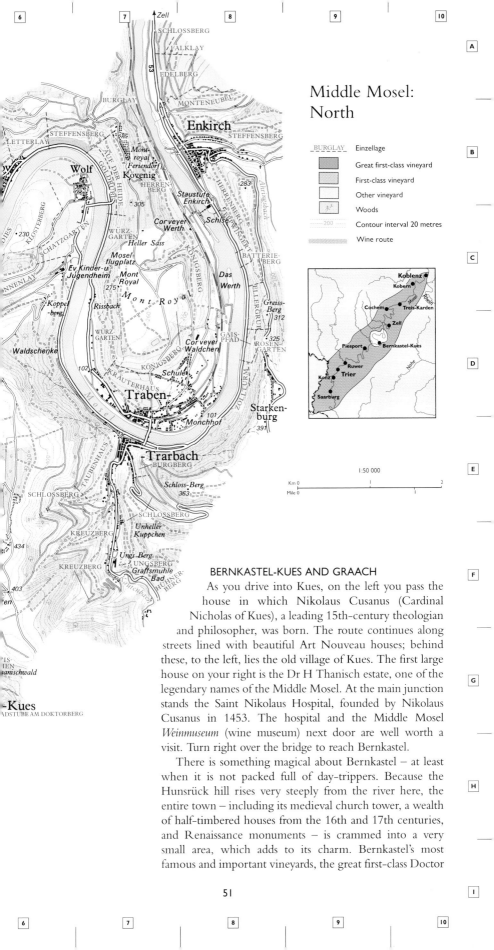

As you drive into Kues, on the left you pass the house in which Nikolaus Cusanus (Cardinal Nicholas of Kues), a leading 15th-century theologian and philosopher, was born. The route continues along streets lined with beautiful Art Nouveau houses; behind these, to the left, lies the old village of Kues. The first large house on your right is the Dr H Thanisch estate, one of the legendary names of the Middle Mosel. At the main junction stands the Saint Nikolaus Hospital, founded by Nikolaus Cusanus in 1453. The hospital and the Middle Mosel *Weinmuseum* (wine museum) next door are well worth a visit. Turn right over the bridge to reach Bernkastel.

There is something magical about Bernkastel – at least when it is not packed full of day-trippers. Because the Hunsrück hill rises very steeply from the river here, the entire town – including its medieval church tower, a wealth of half-timbered houses from the 16th and 17th centuries, and Renaissance monuments – is crammed into a very small area, which adds to its charm. Bernkastel's most famous and important vineyards, the great first-class Doctor

BERNKASTEL-KUES

RECOMMENDED PRODUCERS

Weingüter J Wegeler Erben (Deinhard)
Martertal 2
D 54470 Bernkastel-Kues
Tel: (06531) 2493
During recent years, winemaker Norbert Breit has significantly improved quality at this well-known estate. By appointment only.

Weingut Wwe Dr H Thanisch
Saarallee 31
D 54470 Bernkastel-Kues
Tel: (06531) 2282
Legendary estate with erratic quality in recent years. By appointment only; closed weekends.

Weingut Dr Loosen
St Johannishof
D 54470 Bernkastel
Tel: (06531) 3426
Ernst Loosen runs one of the great estates of Germany, making concentrated, highly expressive wines from top sites of Bernkastel, Graach, Wehlen, Erden and Urzig. Strictly by appointment.

Weingut Dr Pauly Bergweiler and Weingut Peter Nicolay
Gestade 15
D 54470 Bernkastel
Tel: (06531) 3002
During shop opening hours, a selection of the estate's wines can be tasted in the wine shop (above address). The Peter Nicolay wines from Erden and Urzig are usually best.

Weingut Lauerburg
D 54470 Bernkastel
Tel: (06531) 2481
Produces racy wines from Bernkastel's best vineyards. Go to the Lauerburg shop on Bernkastel's Marktplatz.

HOTELS

Hotel zur Post
Gestade 17
D 54470 Bernkastel
Tel: (06531) 2022
Bernkastel's most stylish and comfortable hotel. Rooms facing the street can be loud.

RESTAURANTS

Hoffmann's Weinstube
Bahnhofstrasse 6
D 54470 Bernkastel-Kues
Tel: (06531) 2575
This simple but pleasant restaurant in Kues is a welcome relief from the crowds of tourists and crazy prices all too frequently found on the opposite bank of the Mosel.

and its neighbours the Graben and Lay, rise directly behind the town. Their elegant, refined wines have made Bernkastel's name; the Rieslings from the other surrounding vineyards tend to be firm and slightly earthy.

If you want to explore Bernkastel's narrow, cobbled streets at length, then try to avoid the summer months. The town's wine festival, one of the largest in the Mosel-Saar-Ruwer, takes place during the first weekend in September. Sadly, it is also the high point of Bernkastel's love affair with kitsch, and the wines available at the time are frequently poor. Regardless of the season, however, it is worth making the considerable effort to climb to the ruined castle of Burg Landshut, high above the town (though it is also possible to drive). From here, you can see upstream all the way to Brauneberg, and downstream across the great sea of vines which extends from Bernkastel, past Graach and Wehlen to Zeltingen. This is one of the largest continuous expanses of vines in the Europe.

In Bernkastel itself, the only important estates are those of Dr Pauly-Bergweiler, situated in the imposing grey slate villa on the *Gestade* (promenade) close to the Art Nouveau town hall, and the Lauerburg, whose stylish wine shop is located on Bernkastel's marketplace. The great estate of Dr Loosen lies just outside the town. Take the B53 to reach it and the village of Graach, which lies beyond.

GRAACH

Less than five minutes away from the Bernkastel's hustle and bustle lies Graach, a 'real' wine village less affected by tourism. Here Willi Schaefer is the leading estate, situated right at the beginning of the village's long main street. Behind the spire of Graach's 14th-century church of Saint Andreas looms the Graacher Domprobst, the village's top vineyard site. Fine stone carvings of the stations of the cross stand all along the winding road, which climbs though the vineyard up to the hamlet of Graacher Schäferei. Just outside Graach lies the Josephshof and its vineyard of the same name. Originally owned by the Abbey of Saint Martin in Trier, it has been in the hands of the Reichsgraf von Kesselstatt estate of Trier since church property was secularized by Napoleon during the early 1800s. The rather dilapidated 17th- to 19th-century buildings are currently awaiting a much-needed restoration.

PLACES OF INTEREST

Saint Nikolaus Hospital/ Moselweinmuseum
Bernkastel
The world-famous library of medieval books and Gothic chapel located here are well worth a visit.

Bernkasteler Schweiz
As the B50 climbs into the Hunsrück from Bernkastel, it passes through forests and cliffs, which have become known as 'Bernkastel's Switzerland'.

GRAACH

RECOMMENDED PRODUCERS

Weingut Willi Schaefer
Hauptstrasse 130
D 54470 Graach
Tel: (06531) 8041
Small estate with extremely high standards. Willi Schaefer makes Rieslings of crystalline clarity, with great ageing potential. By appointment only.

Weingut Kees-Kieren
Hauptstrasse 22
D 54470 Graach
Tel: (06531) 3428
Very clean wines with lots of fruit and charm. By appointment only; closed Sunday.

HOTELS

Hotel Panorama
D 54470 Graacher Schäferei
Tel: (06531) 4505
As the name suggests, Albert Kammer's pleasant hotel boasts panoramic views of the Mosel Valley. Fair prices.

RESTAURANTS

Restaurant zum Josephshof
Hauptstrasse 126–8
D 54470 Graach
Tel: (06531) 2272
Simple food of a solid standard and good value. A safer bet than risking the tourist traps of Bernkastel.

Restaurant zur Traube
Hauptstrasse, D 54470 Graach
Tel: (06531) 2189
Traditional restaurant in an attractive old house. Good wines, including older bottles, not featured on the list.

Far left *Bernkastel-Kues, with its stunning situation on one of the Mosel's many loops, has a wealth of fascinating architecture to explore: half-timbered* (top) *and Art Nouveau buildings and* (left) *intriguing Renaissance monuments.*

WEHLEN

From the Josephshof, you can catch the first glimpse of the famous suspension bridge of Wehlen, immortalized on the labels of the village's leading estate, Joh Jos Prüm. Driving up to the bridge, the best parts of the legendary *Sonnenuhr* (sundial) vineyard soar upwards from the road to the right. Although they would appear to enjoy an exposure similar to that of Graach's vineyards, the two villages produce contrasting wines. Graach's best Rieslings are firm and serious, with intense blackcurrant and mineral notes; the wines from the Sonnenuhr are seductively rich, yet supremely delicate. These highly sought-after Rieslings are full of peach and honeysuckle aromas and flavours.

From the bridge there is a fine view of the grand houses of the leading winemakers that line the *Uferallee*, or river-bank street, of Wehlen. A visit to the region would hardly be complete without calling on at least one member of this remarkable collection of estates. Looking back across the vineyards, you can spot the Sonnenuhr which gives its name to the Sonnenuhr vineyard. It was built by Jodocus Prüm in 1842 as a clock for his vineyard workers.

WEHLEN

RECOMMENDED PRODUCERS

Weingut Joh Jos Prüm
Uferallee 19
D 54470 Wehlen
Tel: (06531) 3019
One of great estates of the Mosel – and of Germany as a whole. Dr Manfred Prüm's wines from the top vineyards of Wehlen, Graach and Zeltingen marry intensity with subtlety, and can age for decades. Strictly by appointment.

Weingut Dr F Weins Prüm
Uferallee 20
D 54470 Wehlen
Tel: (06531) 2270
An extremely dependable source for elegant Mosel Rieslings from the top sites of Wehlen, Graach, Erden and Urzig. By appointment only.

Weingut S A Prüm
Uferallee 25–26
D 54470 Wehlen
Tel: (06531) 3110
After a difficult period, Rainmund Prüm is once again making vibrantly fruity, exciting and racy wines. Appointment recommended.

Weingut Heribert Kerpen
Uferallee 6
D 54470 Wehlen
Tel: (06531) 6868
Martin Kerpen's wines are as sleek and as charming as their maker, who produces many fine Spätlesen and Auslesen. By appointment only.

Weingut Studert-Prüm
Hauptstrasse 150
D 54470 Wehlen
Tel: (06531) 2487
Substantial wines from the top vineyards of Wehlen, Graach and Bernkastel, which can lack a little grace. Appointment recommended.

ZELTINGEN

RECOMMENDED PRODUCERS

Weingut Selbach-Oster and Frühmesse Stiftung
Uferallee 23, D 54492 Zeltingen
Tel: (06532) 2081
Johannes Selbach is one of the rising stars of the Mosel. His best wines come from the Zeltinger Sonnenuhr and Graacher Domprobst. By appointment only; closed Sunday.

Weingut Markus Molitor
Haus Klosterberg
D 54470 Zeltingen
Tel: (06532) 3939
What Markus Molitor's wines lack in subtlety they make up for in volume. A big range of BA/TBA. Appointment recommended.

ZELTINGEN

Vineyard sundials are not uncommon in the Middle Mosel; in fact, the next one lies just over a kilometre away, close to Zeltingen. Back on the B53 (heading north) you pass Wehlen's sundial vineyard – which lends its wines the name of Wehlener Sonnenuhr – and then the Sonnenuhr vineyard of Zeltingen, which some experts regard as the equal of its eponymous neighbour. Though Zeltingen is not a particularly interesting village in itself, it is home to the important estate of Selbach-Oster, the only real quality wine estate of the area. Rachtig, another tiny village (it's practically a suburb) situated just north of Zeltingen, boasts but one important monument in the form of the 18th-century *Deutschherrenhof* ('German Manor-house'), which you pass on the right.

HOTELS

Hotel Nicolay zur Post
Uferallee 7, D 54492 Zeltingen
Tel: (06532) 2091
The modern façade is unattractive, but the rooms are comfortable and tasteful. The restaurant is worth a visit.

RESTAURANTS

Restaurant Le Petit (in Hotel St Stephanus)
Uferallee 9, D 54492 Zeltingen
Tel: (06532) 680
Slightly pretentious, but a dependable address.

PLACES OF INTEREST

Kloster Machern
This abbey, now a wine museum and restaurant, is situated on the B53, close to the bridge at Zeltingen. It was founded in the 11th century. The Baroque church is particularly worth seeing.

Left *The famous suspension bridge at Wehlen – travel across this from the town, and you reach one of Germany's most prestigious vineyards, Wehlener Sonnenuhr, home of some of the finest Rieslings.*

Zeltingen has a 'sonnenuhr' vineyard too (above top) *– the sundials were built so pickers did not lose track of time during their vineyard work.*
Above *The riverbank homes of Wehlen's leading winemakers.*

ERDEN

Grey slate is the dominant soil of the Mosel-Saar-Ruwer, but the spectacular view across the river to the massive red cliffs between the great vineyards of Erden and Urzig reveals that this is not exactly the whole story. As elsewhere in the region, the drama of the landscape is reflected in its astonishing wines. No Mosel wines are spicier than the Rieslings produced from the Urziger Würzgarten's red sandstone soil (which stands to reason, given that *Würzgarten* means 'spice garden'), and none are richer, more exotic or seductively tropical than those that come from grapes grown in the red slate of the Erdener Prälat site. The Erdener Treppchen wines are intensely minerally and herbal, with a classical elegance; in these vineyards, there is a mixture of the red and grey slates. Erden itself is a quiet village with a good general standard of wines and one important producer.

URZIG

From Erden, take the bridge over the Mosel and drive slowly in the direction of Urzig (look for the sundial just above the road on the last of the cliffs before the village). Urzig is full of imposing houses that date back to the 16th century. Their presence is an indication of the wealth these

Above *Urzig's grand houses are a fine reflection of the success of its wines and the wealth they bought to the town.*

Above right *Climb Urzig's precipitous vineyards, reaching far above the town, and sensational Mosel Valley views are the reward.*

THE EIFEL

RESTAURANTS

Waldhotel Sonnora
Auf dem Eichelfeld
D 54518 Dreis (near Wittlich)
Tel: (06578) 406
One of Germany's great restaurants. Helmut Thieltge's extremely creative cooking is well worth the 20-minute drive from Zeltingen into the volcanic landscape of the Eifel hills. An excellent wine list, but rather kitschy decor. The hotel rooms are less spectacular, but modestly priced.

ERDEN AND LOSNICH

RECOMMENDED PRODUCERS

Weingut Meulenhof
Zur Kapelle 8
D 54492 Erden
Tel: (06532) 2267
The best wines from Stefan Justen's estate are impressively rich and succulent. By appointment only.

Weingut Stephan Ehlen
Hauptstrasse 21
54492 Lösnich
Tel: (06532) 2388
Slightly erratic estate, capable of making delicate wines from Erden and Lösnich. By appointment only.

URZIG

RECOMMENDED PRODUCERS

Weingut Joh Jos Christoffel Erben
Schanzstrasse 2
D 54539 Urzig
Tel: (06532) 2176
Hans-Leo Christoffel's makes sophisticated, elegant Rieslings from the top vineyards of Erden and Urzig at his small estate. By appointment only.

Weingut Alfred Merkelbach
Brunnenstrasse 11
54539 Urzig
Tel: (06532) 4522
Brothers, Alfred and Rolf Merkelbach, make wines that are full of fruit and 'old-fashioned' in the best sense. By appointment only.

Weingut Jos Christoffel Jr (Christoffel-Prüm)
Moselufer 1
D 54539 Urzig
Tel: (06532) 2113
This estate's wines need years to reach their best, but the list goes back to 1971. By appointment only.

Weingut Moselschild
See hotels.

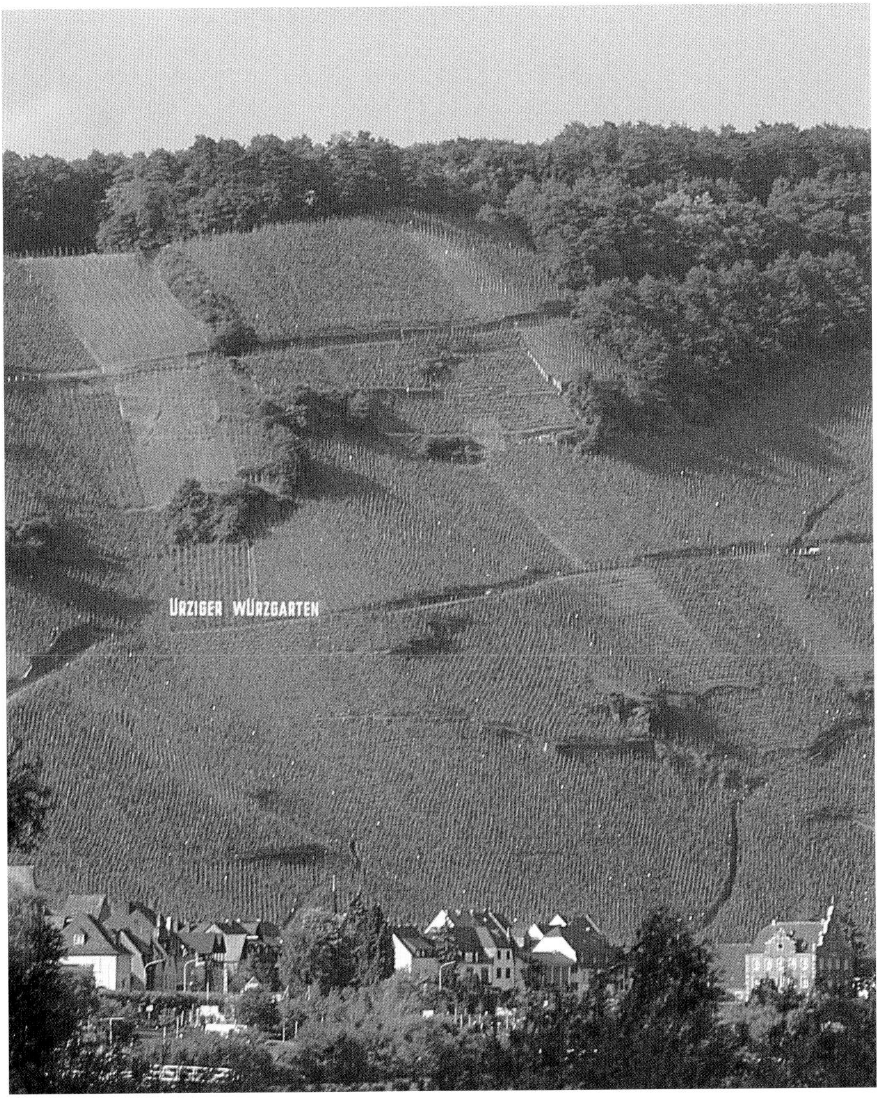

wines brought into the town a century ago. Thanks to the tiny Joh Jos Christoffel estate in the village and the Dr Loosen estate of Bernkastel, the Würzgarten wines are once again highly sought-after today.

To fully appreciate the landscape in this area, take the steep, small road that climbs past the graveyard into the vineyards – but watch out for tractors! Pass the Urziger Würzgarten sign among the vines to come to a viewpoint; here it is possible to take a footpath through the vineyard. The views are sensational, but tread carefully, as there are no handrails. Looking down from these heights, it is easy to imagine that Urzig's remarkable vineyards should make equally remarkable wines.

Return to the bridge at Zeltingen and pass the abbey of Kloster Machern, taking the road signposted Wittlich. From there, join the Autobahn to return to Trier.

HOTELS

Hotel Moselschild
Moselweinstrasse 14
D 54539 Urzig
Tel: (06532) 93930
Urzig's most comfortable hotel also has the best restaurant in this part of the valley. The cooking is old-fashioned, but tasty. The wine list features the Schild family's own good wines, plus some other famous names.

RESTAURANTS

Restaurant Moselschild
See hotels.

TRABEN-TRARBACH

RECOMMENDED PRODUCERS

Weingut Immich-Batterieberg
Im Alten Tal 2
D 56850 Enkirch
Tel: (06541) 9376
After some ups and downs, this estate is once again making good wines. Sabine Basten is the new winemaker. Appointment recommended; closed Sunday.

Albert Kallfelz
Hauptstrasse 60–62
D 56856 Zell-Merl
Tel: (06542) 2713
Zell is best-known for its 'Schwarzer Katz' Grosslage**.** Kallfelz proves that these vineyards can also yield good wines. Closed Saturday afternoon and Sunday.

HOTELS

Rema-Hotel Bellevue
Am Moselufer
D 56841 Traben-Trarbach
Tel: (06541) 7030
Comfortable and stylish hotel designed in 1901 by Art Nouveau master Bruno Möhring, with a good restaurant to boot.

RESTAURANTS

Restaurant Bellevue
See hotels.

Restaurant zur Goldenen Traube
Am Markt 8
D 56841 Traben-Trarbach
Tel: (06541) 6011
This dependable restaurant serves tasty country cooking and sports a good list of local wines.

PLACES OF INTEREST

Mittelmosel-Museum
Traben-Trarbach
Excellent museum documenting the region's chequered history. (Tuesday–Friday 9.30am–noon, 1.30–5pm; Saturday, Sunday 9.30–11am).

PUNDERICH

RECOMMENDED PRODUCERS

Weingut Clemens Busch
Im Wingert 39, D 56862 Pünderich
Tel: (06542) 22180
Makes some of the finest dry Rieslings in the Mosel-Saar-Ruwer area; also the region's leading organic producer. By appointment

TRABEN-TRARBACH AND BEYOND

The twin town of Traben-Trarbach was an important centre of the Mosel wine business a century ago, and the vast wealth earned from this vinous enterprise was ploughed into a remarkable collection of Art Nouveau houses and hotels. The most impressive of these were designed by the Berlin architect Bruno Möhring; his Mosel Bridge of 1899, the Heusgen house of 1904–5 and the Kellerei Julius Kayser of 1907 are particularly fine examples of his work.

The architecture and the picturesque situation of the town, which is located beneath the ruined Grevenburg fortress, make it an ideal destination from Bernkastel (by boat). Today, there are no important wine producers here, but in nearby Enkirch you'll find an historic wine village with one well-known estate: Immich-Batterieberg. The vineyards of Enkirch deserve to be better known, especially as the Batterieberg and Zeppwingert are obvious candidates for classification.

PUNDERICH

Two villages further is Pünderich, whose *Strassenfest* in late September is one of the most attractive street (and wine) festivals in the region. The centre of the village is composed of a beautifully preserved cluster of half-timbered 16th- and 17th-century houses; it is also home to one of the region's best and most characterful winemakers, Clemens Busch. Pünderich's best vineyard, known as the Marienburg, is situated on the opposite bank beneath the castle of the same name. The Mosel flows past the Marienburg on two sides, and from it, there are some magnificent views to be had in both directions.

Traben-Trabach is of greatest importance not for its wines but for its elaborate architecture afforded by trading in them. The Hotel Bellevue (below – interior and exterior views) *is a Bruno Möhring design.*

THE TERRASSEN MOSEL

RECOMMENDED PRODUCERS

Weingut Heymann-Löwenstein
Bahnhofstrasse 10
D 56333 Winningen
Tel: (02606) 1919
Ex-communist Reinhard Löwenstein remains a wine revolutionary. His rich, concentrated, dry Rieslings are excellent, but taste more like Pfalz or Wachau wines. By appointment only.

Weingut Freiherr von Heddesdorf
Haus Heddesdorf
D 56333 Winningen
Tel: (02606) 302
This historic estate makes good wines in fine vintages but they are unreliable in lesser years. By appointment only.

Weingut Stein/ Haus Waldfrieden
Klosterkammerstrasse 14 and Haus Waldfrieden
D 56859 Alf
Tel: (06542) 2979 and 2608
Brothers Peter and Dr Ulrich Stein make a wide range of good, dry and off-dry Rieslings, and excellent Eiswein. By appointment only.

Weingut Reinhold Franzen
Gartenstrasse 14, D 56814 Bremm
Tel: (02675) 412
Ulrich Franzen has made a good name with his polished dry wines from the excellent Neefer Frauenberg site. By appointment only.

Weingut Freiherr von Schleinitz
Kirchstrasse 17
D 56330 Kobern-Gondorf
Tel: (02607) 268
At their best, Konrad Hain's wines are clean, fruity and elegant, but quality has been erratic recently. Appointment recommended.

Weingut Lubentiushof
Kehrstrasse 16
D 56332 Niederfell
Tel: (02607) 8135
Andreas Barth is the new rising star of the Terrassen Mosel, and makes Rieslings with plenty of fruit and character. By appointment only.

RESTAURANTS

Restaurant Burg Thurant
Moselstrasse 16
D 56332 Alken
Tel: (02605) 3581
Peter Kopowski's restaurant in a ferry house from the 14th century is worth visiting for the architecture alone. The food is rustic and hearty.

Above *The town of Zell: nestled between precipitous vineyards and the River Mosel, its medieval buildings cling to narrow terraces just as the vines do.*

Above right *Negotiating the steep slopes is a tricky process for Terrassen vines – growing them upwards on posts, rather than along training wires makes life easier.*

THE TERRASSEN MOSEL

The lower section of the Mosel Valley, particularly downstream from the twin town of Treis-Karden, is a world unto itself. Here the valley is rockier and less convoluted, and the vines cling to the narrow terraces which sit on the precipitous valley sides. Hence the name *Terrassen*, or terraces (of the) Mosel. The region's appeal is added to by a wealth of medieval architecture; the most prominent example is Burg Eltz, the only important castle in the Mosel Valley to escape destruction during the many wars of the 17th and 18th centuries.

The most important winemaking communities – both in terms of quantity and quality – are Winningen and Kobern-Gondorf. Both are only a quarter of an hour's

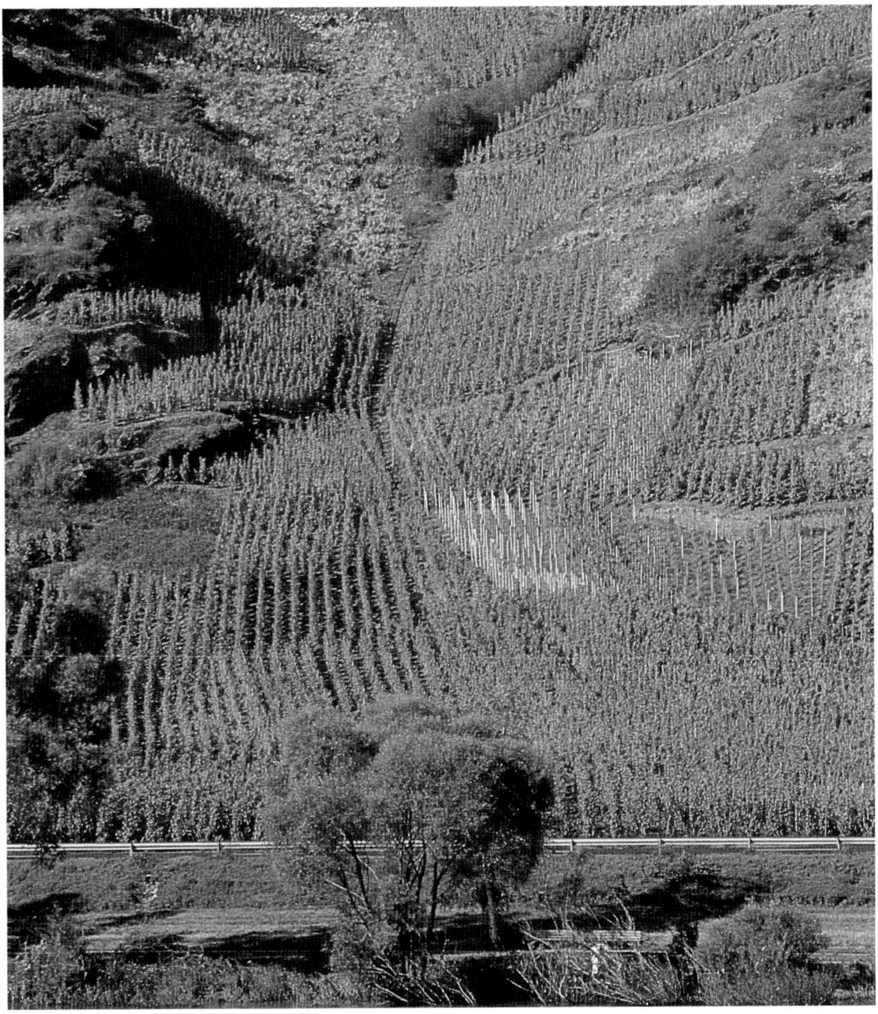

drive from Koblenz (or the Koblenz/Dieblich exit from the A61 Autobahn if you are travelling further afield). Winningen is home to the area's leading producer, Heymann-Löwenstein, and to the von Heddesdorf estate; there is also a miniature 'castle' in the centre of town. Between the two towns lies the Terrassen Mosel's finest vineyard: the breathtaking Winninger Uhlen. While its extremely narrow terraces rise steeply from the river bank, the surprisingly graceful arch of the bridge that spans the entire valley lends the scene something of a surreal quality. Kobern has two ruined castles and the late Romanesque *Matthiaskapelle* (Chapel of Saint Matthew), believed to have been built over the burial site of Saint Matthew's skull.

From Kobern, it is about an hour to Burg Eltz: a 20-minute drive up the river past castles and dramatic rock formations to the village of Müden, and from there, a 40-minute climb on foot. Exhausting though the latter might be, there could certainly be no more fitting conclusion to any tour of the Mosel-Saar-Ruwer.

Restaurant Halterschenke
Hauptstrasse 63, D 56332 Dieblich
Tel: (02607) 1008
This attractive restaurant on the right bank of the Mosel offers good country cooking and moderately priced regional wines.

PLACES OF INTEREST

Beilstein
Extremely picturesque village, with ruined castle of the von Metternich family (later owners of the Rheingau's Schloss Johannisberg).

Burg Eltz
Moselkern/Müden
The historic interiors of the Mosel Valley's best preserved medieval castle can be viewed only on guided tours (every quarter of an hour, April 1–November 1, Monday–Friday 9am–5.30pm, Saturday and Sunday 10am–5.30pm).

Koblenz

KOBLENZ

RECOMMENDED PRODUCERS

Deinhard & Co (Weingut Geheimrat J Wegeler Erben)
Deinhardplatz
D 56068 Koblenz
Tel: (0261) 1040
Deinhard is the largest vineyard owner in Germany, with 100ha of vineyards in the Mosel-Saar-Ruwer, Pfalz and Rheingau. The wines from these estates are marketed under the J Wegeler name in order to distance them from Deinhard's Sekt business. Appointments to visit the estates can be made directly with the estates or through the head office.

HOTELS

Diehls Hotel
Am Pfaffendorfer Tor 10
D 56077 Koblenz
Tel: (0261) 56077
Diehls is a comfortable hotel with fine views of the Rhine and Koblenz's Schloss.

Almost any tour through the Mosel and Rhine regions passes through Koblenz. Koblenz was once one of the most beautiful cities on the Rhine; now it (unjustly) enjoys the reputation for being one of the most boring. It suffered terribly in numerous wars: after the Thirty Years War, only half the buildings were left standing; the French bombardment during the Pfalz War of Succession in 1688 left most of the town damaged; and in 1945, only 17 percent of the buildings remained intact. Since then, however, the historic heart of the city has been lovingly restored. The city and the great fortress of Ehrenbreitstein, immortalized in William Turner's paintings, make it well worth a stop.

The most prominent sight in Koblenz is the huge monument to Kaiser Wilhelm I, who was inaugurated in 1897. Love its grandeur or loathe its Wilhelmine pomposity, you cannot avoid it. Behind it stand three massive sections of the Berlin Wall, a memorial to those who suffered as a result of the division of Germany following the Second World War. To make the contrast of styles even more extraordinary, next to these monuments is the reconstructed Rhein Wing of the Deutschherrenhaus (originally late-Gothic, then remodelled in the

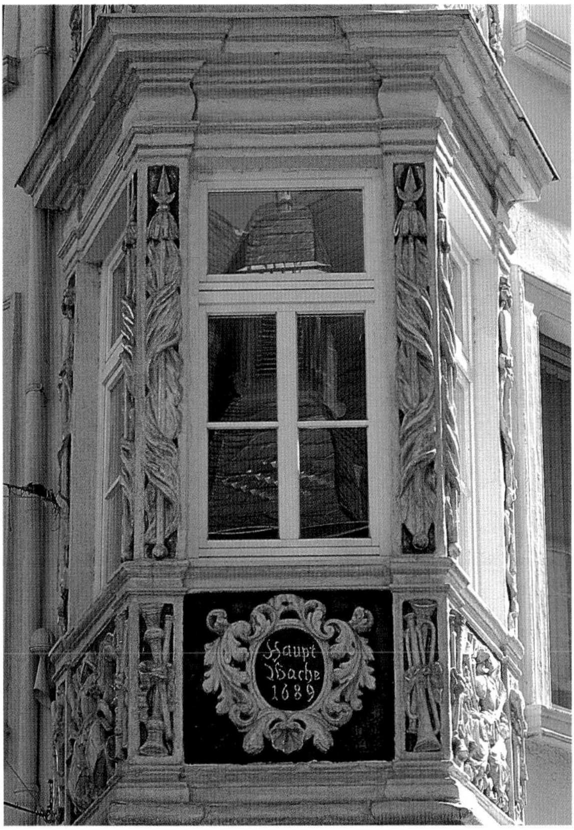

Left *Koblenz has a great many fine old buildings, too many to list, but a walk around the Altstadt reveals some of the finest – this one is on the marketplace.*
Far left *The Prussian-designed Ehrenbreitstein building (re-styled in the early 1800s) is one of the largest fortifications in Germany – it has spectacular views over the Koblenz area.*

Baroque style) and the Romanesque church of Saint Kastor. The latter was consecrated in 836AD; the last sections of the four-towered structure were completed in 1499.

A short walk along the bank of the Rhine leads to the gardens below the *Schloss* (castle or palace), designed by landscape architect Peter Lenée. The palace itself, the region's first significant example of neo-classical architecture, was completed just eight years before its builder Prince-Bishop Clemens Wenzeslaus and his clerical administration were toppled by the Napoleonic invasion of 1794.

The Prussian government that followed the Congress of Vienna in 1815 turned Ehrenbreitstein (on the opposite bank) into one of the largest fortifications in Germany. It now houses the Landesmuseum Koblenz, the Rheinmuseum (which documents the history of traffic on the river) and the local youth hostel. From here, there are commanding views of the surrounding area.

The narrow streets between the Schloss and the Mosel – the heart of the Altstadt – deserve the most attention. There are too many fine buildings to mention them all, but the tower-like Deutscher Kaiser Haus, (early 16th century), the elegant *Dreikönigenhaus* ('House of the Three Kings; 1701) on Kornpfortstrasse, and the *Alte Kaufhaus* (Old Merchant Exchange; 1724) on the corner of Kastorstrasse and Kornpfortstrasse, should not be missed.

RESTAURANTS

Historischer Weinkeller
Mehlgasse 16
D 56068 Koblenz
Tel: (0261) 14626
This exceptional wine bar is located in a vaulted 13th-century cellar, and offers a carefully picked selection of wines from all 13 of Germany's winegrowing regions, complemented by a regional specialities.

Restaurant Loup de Mer
Neustadt 12
D 56068 Koblenz
Tel: (0261) 16138
As the name suggests, Loup is a fish restaurant concentrating on the fruits of the sea rather than those of the local rivers. Good wine list.

Restaurant Stresemann
Rheinzollstrasse 8
D 56068 Koblenz
Tel: (0261) 15464
A bistro restaurant serving good country cooking in ample portions. Unexceptional wines.

PLACES OF INTEREST

Stolzenfels
The ruined medieval castle of Stolzenfels was rebuilt by the architect Schinkel for the Prussian Crown Prince (later King) Friedrich Wilhelm IV in 1836–42, taking great care to preserve as much of the original structure as possible.

The Ahr

The Ahr is one of the most beautiful and charming winemaking regions in Germany. What distinguishes it from nearby winemaking areas is the fact that 85 percent of its vineyards are planted with red grapes – even though the sites are among the country's most northern. This is a relic from pre-17th-century days, when red wine was important for virtually all of Germany's winemaking regions, surviving even the white-wine boom of the 19th and 20th centuries. That the dominance of red grapes should have survived is partly an historical accident and partly due to the warm microclimate that characterizes the Upper Ahr Valley between Walporzheim and Kreuzberg. When the sun shines here, temperatures rise very fast, and the stony slate soils make an extremely effective heat reservoir. This enables red grapes, particularly the Spätburgunder, to ripen remarkably well over a warm summer.

There is a fine view of the region's most eastern vineyards from the A61 Autobahn where it crosses the Ahr Valley. To reach the Ahr's most important winemaking communities, take the Bad Neuenahr exit, then follow the B267 past the twin town of Bad Neuenahr-Ahrweiler to Walprozheim, where the Upper Ahr begins. There are many sheltered south-facing sites in this narrow, twisting stretch of the valley; the less-favoured slopes are clothed in forests, creating a scene that could hardly be more picturesque.

Sadly, the beauty of the landscape is not always reflected in its wines. In spite of a winemaking revolution during the last decade, too many of the region's red wines are still pale, acidic and lacking in fruit and depth. For a long time, the natural beauty of the Ahr region and its proximity to Bonn

The Ahr is one of Germany's most beautiful wine regions and there are few more fittingly attractive towns to complement the landscape than Ahrweiler. Its historic centre (left) *is still surrounded by the original town walls. The region is renowned more for red than white wines – some of the best are found in casks at the Meyer-Näkel estate* (above).

THE AHR

RECOMMENDED PRODUCERS

Weingut Meyer Näkel
Hardtbergstrasse 20
D 53507 Dernau
Tel: (02643) 1628
Self-taught winemaker Werner Näkel makes the most sophisticated Spätburgunder reds in the Ahr: Pinot Noirs that marry pure fruit with subtle oak. Top wines are sold either as Auslese Trocken or under the 'S' and Blauschiefer names. Strictly by appointment only.

Weingut Kreuzberg
Benedikt-Schmittmann-Strasse 30
D 53507 Dernau
Tel: (02643) 3206
Up-and-coming estate making good, if rather traditional, wines. The Kreuzberg's *Strasswirtschaft*, or vintner's tavern, is open from 3pm every day except Wednesday between May and October. Appointment recommended for wine tastings.

Weingut Deutzerhof
D 53508 Mayschoss
Tel: (02643) 7264
Wolfgang Hehle is a newcomer to the Ahr, and has recently become a name in the region. He offers big Spätburgunder reds with plenty of tannin and oak; also excellent Rieslings, both in dry and dessert styles. Strictly by appointment.

Weingut Sonnenberg (Görres & Linden)
Heerstrasse 98
D 53474 Bad Neuenahr
Tel: (02641) 6713
Young estate with slightly erratic quality, but some serious reds. Appointment recommended.

Weingut Toni Nelles
Göppinger Strasse 13
D 53474 Heimersheim
Tel: (02641) 24349
The labels of the Nelles wines announce that their involvement in viticulture goes back to 1479. Today, they decorate bottles of light but attractive Spätburgunder red and rosé wines. Also runs Weinhaus Nelles, a restaurant specializing in regional cooking, and a small hotel.

HOTELS

Steigenberger Kurhotel
Kurgartenstrasse 1
D 53474 Bad Neuenahr
Tel: (02641) 9410
Grand and luxurious hotel with excellent bar and Viennese-style café. There is also a swimming pool and direct access to the spa baths.

and Cologne compensated for these deficiencies. Even with poor red wines it was once easy for winemakers to make a good living. But the German government's move from Bonn to Berlin is sounding the death-knell for business here.

Stop in Dernau at Meyer Näkel, or in Deutzerhof in idyllic Mayschoss, and you find red wines at the opposite end of the quality scale: not as big or powerful as the best Pinot Noirs from Baden or the Pfalz, but full of cherry and dark berry fruits, with plenty of tannins integrated into an elegant whole. Both the Meyer Näkel and Deutzerhof winemakers have mastered the use of new oak *barriques* for maturing their wines, which can be classed among Germany's new red-wine elite. Several of their colleagues

are beginning to catch up, so that the region now has half-a-dozen serious red-wine producers. Be prepared, though: good Ahr red wines begin at about DM20 (£9) per bottle direct from the winegrower.

It is something of a mystery as to why exciting Riesling wines are such a rarity in the Ahr. Anyone familiar with the Mosel-Saar-Ruwer will immediately notice how the Ahr's best vineyards resemble those of the Mosel. At present, the best Rieslings come from Deutzerhof, which has produced some astonishing Riesling Eisweins and Trockenbeeren-auslesen recently. This could be the beginning of a new trend, but don't expect much from the majority of white wines you are offered here.

RESTAURANTS

Steinheuers Restaurant zur alten Post/Landgasthof Poststuben
Landskronerstrasse 110
D 53474 Heppingen
Tel: (02641) 7011
Hans-Peter Steinheuer's creative modern cooking belongs to the best this part of Germany has to offer. Early reservation is strongly recommended. In his Landgasthof the same high standards are maintained, but the cooking is more traditional.

Restaurant Alt Sinzig
Kölner Strasse 5
D 53489 Sinzig
Tel: (02642) 42757
An idiosyncratic mix of local and Normandy-style cooking makes Jean-Marie Dumaine's restaurant like no other in the area. Very fair prices.

Restaurant Brogsitter
Walporzheimer Strasse 134b
D 53474 Walporzheim
Tel: (02641) 97750
A medieval house turned into a fine restaurant. The food isn't adventurous, but of dependably good quality. Avoid the Brogsitter estate's wines.

Wein-Gasthaus-Schäferkarre
Brückenstrasse 29, D 53505 Altenahr
Tel: (02643) 7128
This Weinstube is in a beautifully restored winemaker's house (1716) and has an extensive list of local wines.

PLACES OF INTEREST

Ahrweiler
Though hidden in the spa town of Bad Neuenahr-Ahrweiler, the historic heart of Ahrweiler is beautifully preserved. The 14th- and 15th-century Gothic church of St-Laurentius and Rococo *Rathaus* (town hall) also merit attention.

Bad Neuenahr
The golden age of this spa town was the late-19th and early-20th centuries. The Art Nouveau spa house is particularly impressive.

Remagen
The Remagener *Brücke* (bridge) was the first crossing point over the Rhine for Allied troops in 1945. On the March 17, it unexpectedly collapsed. The remaining towers have been turned into a museum.

Sinzig
The church of St-Peter is one of the most outstanding buildings in this part of Germany.

The natural beauty of the Ahr is beyond question, but any vineyard landscape looks bleaker in the winter – a punctuation of whitewashed houses (left) *adds brightness.*

The Mittelrhein

The Rhine Gorge, situated between Koblenz and Bingen, is what most people think of as the quintessential Rhine. Postcards of the craggy Loreley, romantic castles, vineyards and the works of romantic poets and painters such as Heinrich Heine and William Turner have made this part of the Rhine's long course from the Alps to the North Sea the section that has stuck in people's minds. Frequently, visitors arrive imagining this area to be the Rheingau, and are greatly surprised to discover that this stretch of the Rhein is actually the *Mittelrhein* (Middle Rhine region), a name many have never heard before.

The Mittelrhein has many strengths, including its natural beauty and wealth of architectural monuments from the Middle Ages and the Renaissance. It has more castles than the Rheingau, and its scenery is every bit as dramatic and beautiful as the Mosel. It also produces a lot of good wine, but what it lacks are world-famous estates such as Schloss Johannisberg, Langwerth von Simmern, Joh Jos Prüm or Maximin Grünhaus. Indeed, much of its production is sold in bulk for sparkling-wine production, ending up in products such as Deinhard's Lila Riesling Sekt, which does not mention the Mittelrhein at all on its label. In the last few years, only Toni Jost's estate in Bacharach has begun to acquire an international reputation.

This means that even the region's best wines are modestly priced, in spite of the high production costs incurred because of the region's steep, rocky vineyards. But the Mittelrhein's top estates are just beginning to achieve real success, which should encourage young winemakers to improve quality. There is plenty to discover. For this reason it is a good idea to steer clear of the most touristy towns and villages and explore elsewhere. It is ideal country for wine prospectors.

Left and above *This tower was built in the 14th century by the lords of Gutenfels Castle – its construction here, in the middle of the River Rhine, was strategically to collect tolls from passing river traffic.*

Mittelrhein

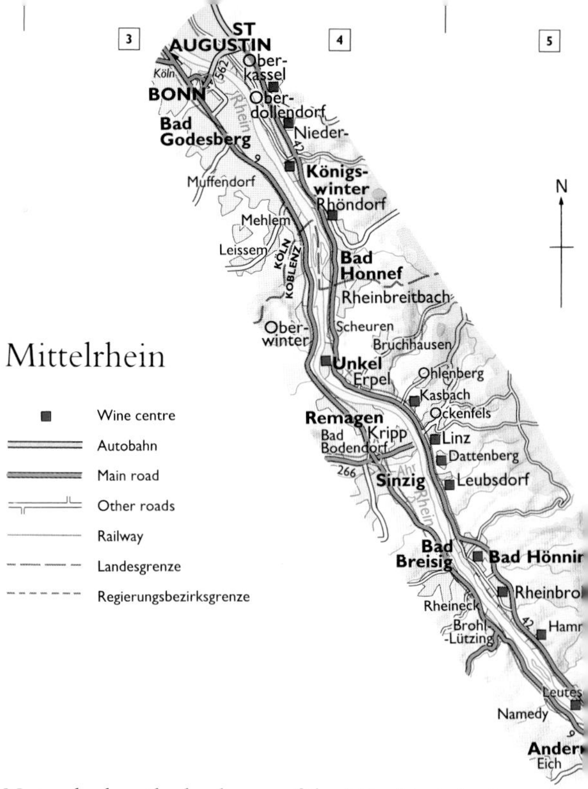

Not only does the landscape of the Mittelrhein look like that of the Mosel on a grander, more imposing scale, but the region's Riesling wines are also similar but bigger in style. The combination of the narrow river valley microclimate and the vineyards' stony slate soils is what creates this family resemblance. The slightly warmer climate of the Rhine Valley, due mainly to the broader expanse of the river (water being a very effective heat reservoir) often gives the wines extra body and richness and makes their acidity slightly less pointed than that found in Mosel Rieslings.

However, not only does the northern half of the Mittelrhein offer fewer dramatic landscapes, it is also less exciting vinously. This is because the breadth of the Rhine River here, while trapping heat when the sun shines, also lets in larger amounts of cool air; only on the river's right bank are the slopes actually sunny enough to allow Riesling to ripen. While some of the best vineyards are located in Leuesdorf, just north of Neuwied, the most attractive Mittelrhein wines actually come from further south, around Boppard, and from the stretch of the Rhine that runs between the Loreley cliffs and the Mittelrhein's southern tip. Their potential is worth watching.

Of all the German wine regions it is the Mittelrhein that is most associated with romantic river cruises and fairytale castles – such as that at St-Goarshausen (below).

THE MITTELRHEIN

Above The Rhine Valley and the towns of Pfalzgrafenstein and Gutenfels. The surrounding wine estates are good, but few are famous – much of their wine is made into sparkling Sekt.

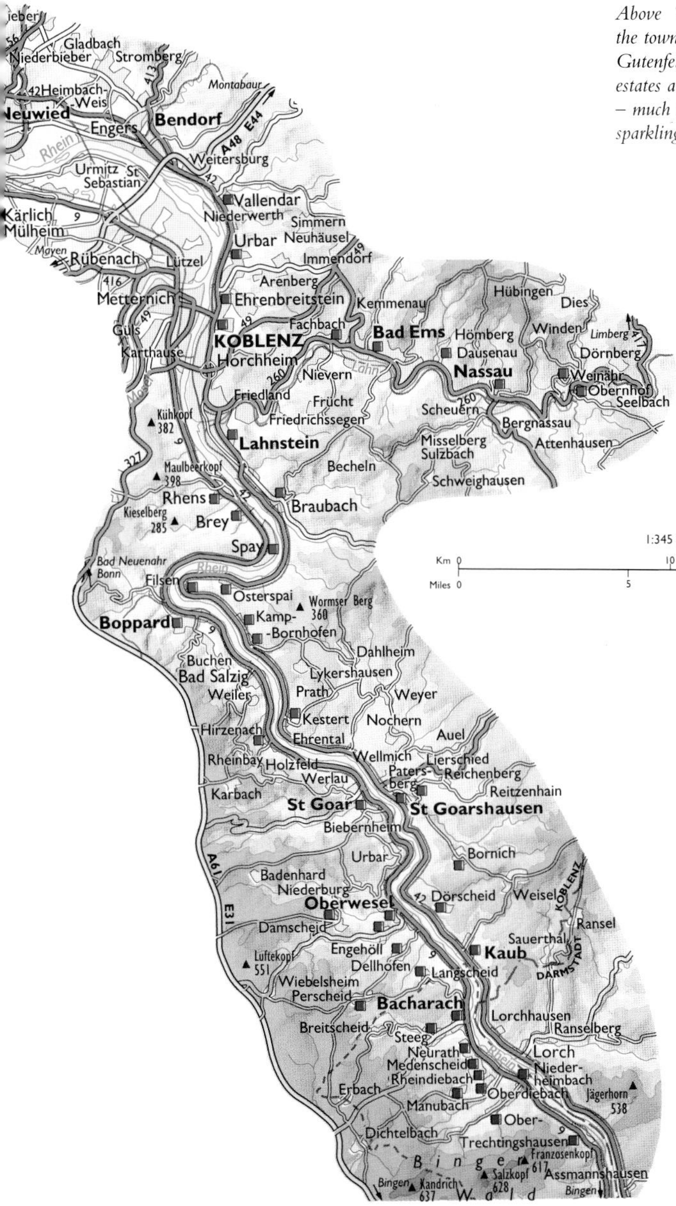

1:345 000
Km 0 10 20
Miles 0 5 10

BOPPARD AND SPAY

RECOMMENDED PRODUCERS

Weingut August Perll
Oberstrasse 81
D 56154 Boppard
Tel: (06742) 3906
Makes solid Rieslings from Bopparder Hamm. In good vintages, the Spätlesen and Auslesen are fine.

Weingut Walter Perll
Ablassgasse 11
D 56154 Boppard
Tel: (06742) 3671
Rather erratic wines, but when Walter Perll is on target his Rieslings are brimming with fruit and have a Mosel-like elegance.

Weingut Heinrich Müller
Mainzer Strasse 45
D 56322 Spay
Tel: (02628) 8741
Young Matthias Müller has rapidly become the leading producer of Bopparder Hamm Rieslings. His are racy wines with more depth than those from other producers. Appointment recommended.

Weingut Adolf Weingart
Mainzer Strasse 32
D 56322 Spay
Tel: (02628) 8735
Few really exciting wines, but has an extremely dependable source of Boppard wines offering good value for money across the board.

HOTELS

Hotel Bellevue
Rheinallee 41
D 56154 Boppard
Tel: (06742) 1020
Boppard's finest hotel, situated directly on the bank of the Rhine, with swimming pool and sauna.

Golfhotel Jakobsberg
D 56154 Boppard
Tel: (06742) 8080
This comfortable hotel, with its own 18-hole golf course, tennis courts, swimming pool and gymnasium, is best reached from Spay. It is located 10km north of Boppard.

PLACES OF INTEREST

Rhens
Much of the extensive town wall and the fortifying towers of Rhens remain intact; however it is the *Königsstuhl* (the king's seat) that is the town's most important sight. This stone platform upon which Germany's Prince-Bishops met to choose the nation's kings was completed in 1398. The present Königsstuhl is a copy made at the request of Prussian King Friedrich Wilhelm IV.

BOPPARD

Anyone with the faintest appreciation of wine will not fail to be impressed by the vast amphitheatre of vines that makes up the Bopparder Hamm vineyards. Here, the only major loop in the Rhine's course through the Mittelrhein creates one of the best vineyards along the entire river. Although no Roman wine-presses have been excavated here as in Brauneberg, Piesport and Erden on the Mosel, the remaining walls of the Roman fort in the centre of town reveal Boppard's importance during the latter period of Roman rule. Wine production played a significant role here during the 12th and 13th centuries. The twin-spired, late-Romanesque church of Saint Severus also dates back to this period.

The most prominent feature of the town is the row of grand hotels that lines the Rheinallee on the river-bank. Boppard's long-standing popularity as a tourist destination accounts for the town's prosperity. But while the area can boast a handful of reliable producers who make Bopparder Hamm Rieslings, moments of brilliance are rather rare. Competition among local vintners to supply the local

hotels and restaurants has kept the price of Bopparder Hamm wines low compared with those of similar quality elsewhere. Even at the Heinrich Müller estate, the town's leading producer, not a single Riesling Spätlese costs more than DM10 (£4.50). On the one hand, this means you get some of the best value for money in Germany, but on the other, it makes it economically unviable to keep to low yields and selective harvesting which would fully exploit the potential of these great vineyards.

When Bopparder Hamm Rieslings are good they are the most aromatic of all Mittelrhein wines, combining a silky richness with a crispness of palate. The Bopparder Hamm is sub-divided into seven separate sites, with the Ohlenberg, Feuerlay and Mandelstein vineyards constituting the best areas of its great sweep. Many of the best wines can be found in the cellars of winemakers in Boppard and Spay, just to the north. The peak of tourist season is late summer, so unless you like crowds, do not explore the narrow streets of Boppard's Altstadt at this time. However, don't miss highlights such as the imposing Ritter-Schwalbach-Haus at the eastern end of the Rheinallee.

Above left *The vineyards of Bopparder Hamm – one of the best sites along the River Rhine. Despite their wonderful potential, wines from these vines do not reach high prices.*
Above right *Bopparder Hamm is divided into seven different sites: each is beautifully tended and even the smallest patch of space used.*

BACHARACH

RECOMMENDED PRODUCERS

Weingut Toni Jost
Oberstrasse 14, D 55420 Bacharach
Tel: (06743) 1216
Peter and Linde Jost's estate remains number one in the Mittelrhein, making rich, aromatic Rieslings that always retain their makers' charm. Appointment recommended; closed Saturday and Sunday mornings.

Dr Randolph Kauer
Mainzer Strasse 21,
D 55422 Bacharach
Tel: (06743) 2272
It took less than five years for Randolph Kauer to make his small, organic estate one of Bacharach's best. Intensely minerally wines with excellent ageing potential.

Weingut Fritz Bastian
Oberstrasse 63
D 55422 Bacharach
Tel: (06743) 1208
Erratic producer, capable of making fine wines from the famous Posten vineyard. The wine bar is open from noon until midnight every day except Thursday; otherwise by appointment.

Weingut Ratzenberger
Blücherstrasse 167
D 55422 Steeg
Tel: (06743) 1337
Ratzenberger's Rieslings are classic Mittelrhein wines capable of long ageing. Some have been less polished, but there is a high general standard. Appointment recommended.

Weingut Mades
Borbachstrasse 35–36
D 55422 Steeg
Tel: (06743) 1449
Helmut Mades makes substantial Rieslings with plenty of fruit and character. The Mades' Strausswirtschaft is open from Friday to Sunday, March through to late October; otherwise by appointment only.

Weingut Lanius-Knab
Mainzer Strasse 38
D 55430 Oberwesel
Tel: (06744) 8104
Crystal-clear, steely Rieslings have rapidly established this estate as one of the Mittelrhein's top ten. By appointment only; closed Sunday.

HOTELS

Burghotel Auf Schönburg
D 55430 Oberwesel
Tel: (06744) 7027
Perched 230m above Oberwesel, this fine hotel within the remains of a ancient castle could not be better situated.

BACHARACH

Though Bacharach currently offers the most exciting wines of the region and is packed full of history, it is worth taking time to get there. A short distance south from Boppard along the B9, and on the opposite bank (a ferry links the two), lie Saint Goar and its twin town of Saint Goarshausen. Both are worth a visit before continuing past the cliffs of the Loreley to Oberwesel.

Oberwesel has been through tremendous change in its history, including the first artillery bombardment on the Rhine in 1390, and the terrible destruction caused by the Thirty Years War and the Palatinate War of Succession in the 17th century. In spite of these events, many fine old buildings remain, including the beautiful Gothic *Liebfrauenkirche* (Church of Our Lady) and several of the towers which once fortified the town's walls. In Lanius-Knab, Oberwesel has finally found a producer with the ability to rebuild its name as a leading wine town. But on the opposite bank lies Kaub, a depressing example of the region's current state. As yet, no one is taking advantage of the fine Rosstein and Backofen vineyard sites to make quality Rieslings.

Further south along the B9 lies Bacharach, which stands where one of the many valleys running down from the Hunsrück meets the Rhine. Like many Mittelrhein wine towns, Bacharach stretches along the narrow strip of reasonably flat ground along the river-bank. The narrow, cobbled *Oberstrasse* (Upper Street), home to the Toni Jost estate, runs the entire length of the town. Near the northern

end of the late-Romanesque church of Saint Peter lies the finest of the town's many old buildings: the half-timbered *Altes Haus* (literally 'Old House'; 1568) and the slightly later Zum Grünen Baum (the *Weinstube*, or wine-tavern, of the Fritz Bastian estate); above them stands the ruined Gothic Wernerkapelle, which was completed in 1426.

Nearly all Bacharach's best wines come from the valley's south-facing vineyards, which climb from Bacharach up to the village of Steeg and the Helmut Mades and Ratzenberger estates. There is a timeless quality to Steeg, which, though only two kilometres from the Rhine, seems a world away from its traffic. On the opposite side of the Steeg Valley from the vineyards runs the still-discernible path of a Roman road that once crossed the Hunsrück to Trier. The Rieslings from these vineyards can have a steely acidity and, while often unforthcoming when young, can blossom magnificently after several years' of age. The best live for decades. Those from the Steeg's Saint Jost site are the most minerally and austere, those from Bacharach's Posten vineyard are the most aromatic and succulent, and those from the Wolfshöhle lie between the two extremes.

Close to Bacharach are several other notable vineyards, chiefly the Hahn, just to the north. Virtually a monopoly of the Toni Jost estate, it yields the most intense, powerful Rieslings of the entire Mittelrhein. At Bacharach's southern edge, in the imposing buildings that once contained the important wine house of Wasum, is the Randolph Kauer estate. A short distance out of town in this direction lies the fine Fürstenburg vineyard of Oberdiebach, beneath its ruined castle; again, the best wines here are made by Toni Jost. From the castle there is a fine view of Lorch and the northern tip of the Rheingau on the Rhine's opposite bank.

Far left *The Alte Haus – one of Bacharach's most beautiful buildings: there are many to discover and they are not hard to find as the town only has a relatively small and narrow piece of land to occupy* (above), *tucked between the river and hills.*

Schlosshotel und Villa Rheinfels
Schlossberg 47, D 56329 Saint Goar
Tel: (06741) 8020
Comfortable hotel, with magnificent views, housed in a castle high above the Rhine. Swimming pool and sauna.

RESTAURANTS

Historische Weinwirtschaft
Liebfrauenstrasse 17
D 55430 Oberwesel
Tel: (06744) 8186
A beautiful 500-year-old house, authentic regional cooking and good local wines all make Iris Marx's restaurant worth a long detour.

PLACES OF INTEREST

Kaub
The imposing Toll castle of Pfalzgrafenstein is worth the boat trip (daily tours), though the views of it from the river are more impressive.

Saint Goar/Saint Goarshausen
The massive ruins of the Rheinfels castle high above Saint Goar now house a hotel. The famous Loreley cliffs are best reached from Saint Goarshausen on the opposite bank of the Rhine.

The Nahe

Anyone who knows the Nahe region and its best wines will find it strange that, among Germans, it is the least well-known of the country's winegrowing regions – especially considering that not only does the Nahe Valley boast some spectacular scenery, its best Rieslings are among the finest wines available. While many of the Nahe's great vineyards have a long history, the problem is that the borders of the region were only properly drawn in 1971. The valley of the Nahe – stretching from the river's confluence with the Rhine at Bingen upstream to Monzingen – is the water source for the wines that have given the region an excellent name among wine enthusiasts worldwide. All kinds of wines are produced in the valleys of the Nahe's tributaries (the Guldenbach, Gräfenbach, Ellerbach, Glan and Alsenz) and these also bear the Nahe name. Some are very good, but many bear little resemblance to wines from the heart of the region. The Nahe, in effect, has an identity problem.

The desire to give the Nahe its own identity often means that its wines are described as being halfway between those of the Mosel and Rheingau. There is a certain amount of truth in this, because Nahe Rieslings are highly aromatic – like Mosel wines – but with more body, thus resembling those of the Rheingau. However, this generalization ignores what makes the region's best wines so distinctive: a fascinating, intensely minerally character. This characteristic comes from the volcanic soils and the crystal-laden porphyry and melaphyre rocks, great chunks of which protrude from the vineyards. The rocks and cliffs that punctuate the landscape of the Nahe give the region its distinctive appearance, and the wines their singularity.

Visitors with limited time should concentrate on the Nahe Valley itself. It is divided into four sections: the Lower Nahe from Bingerbrück to Bretzenheim; the area directly around Bad Kreuznach; the Middle Nahe from Bad Münster

Left *The Luitpoldbrücke at Oberhausen, spanning the river to reach some of the town's best vineyards: the Nahe region has some fine ones. Bad Kreuznach* (above) *is the natural starting point for exploring the area.*

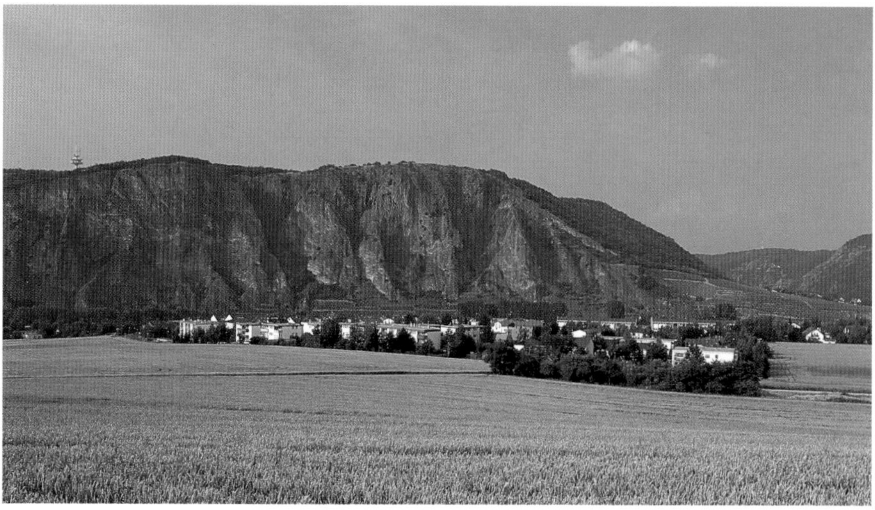

to Schlossböckelheim; and the Upper Nahe beyond Schlossböckelheim (Alsenz is the most important of the tributary valleys). Each of these areas produces rather different wines, but all are capable of greatness.

The various sub-areas do not shine with equal brightness, however, primarily because several of the big estates, which once gave the region its international reputation, no longer live up to their former high standards. Today, as in so many other regions in Germany, it is small, family-owned estates that stand at the forefront, most notably Dönnhoff, Schlossgut Diel, Crusius and Emrich-Schönleber.

It is extraordinary to discover the degree of precision with which wines in the Nahe Valley reflect the contours of the landscape in which they grow: the more dramatic the scenery, the more complex the wines. No other German wines better reflect the concept of *terroir*. The virtual absence of tourists only adds to the Nahe's appeal; its valleys seem so far removed from the city of Frankfurt, yet they are just under an hour's drive away. The Middle and Upper Nahe offer absolute quiet for those seeking tranquility – this, and some magnificent Rieslings.

Above *The striking red Rotenfels cliffs, rising 200 metres above the Bad Münster countryside – the very fine Traiser Bastei vineyard at their foot also brings fame to the region.*

Left *Hotels and restaurants a plenty add to Bad Kreuznach's convenience and charm, but it has a wealth of intriguing sites and architecture to discover too.*

Nahe

Wine centre
Autobahn
Main road
Other roads
Railway
Landesgrenze
Regierungsbezirksgrenze
1:200 000
Km 0 2 4 6 8 10
Miles 0 1 2 3 4 5 6
N
Rhein
Bingerbrück
Weiler
Bingen
Kempten
Büdesheim
Mainz
Waldalgesheim
Münster-Sarmsheim
Roth
Genheim
RHEINHESSEN-PFALZ
KOBLENZ
A61 E31
Koblenz
Stromberg
Rümmelsheim
Waldlaubersheim
Burglayen
Dietersheim
Eckenroth
Dorsheim
Sponsheim
Schöneberg
Schweppenhausen
Laubenheim
Schlangebaum 300
Grolsheim
Windesheim
Hergenfeld
Dalberg
Spabrücken
Waldhilbersheim
Langenlonsheim
Gensingen
Grafenbach
Guldental
Heddesheim
Guldenbach
Wallhausen
Gutenberg
Bretzenheim
Ippesheim
Argenschwang
Gauchsberg
Sommerloch
Biebelsheim
Worms
437
Braunweiler
Winzenheim
St.Katharinen
Planig
Roxheim
Hargesheim
Bosenberg 227
Mandel
Sponheim
Rüdesheim
Bad Kreuznach
Bosenheim
Ellerbach
Burgsponheim
Weinsheim
Hüffelsheim
Traisen
Hackenheim
böckelheim
Schlossböckelheim
Bad Münster-Ebernburg
Norheim
303
Niederhausen
Boos
341
336
Oberhausen
Altenbamberg
Duchroth
Feilbingert
Nahe
Fürfeld
Hochstätten
Odernheim
Hallgarten
Glan
Niederhausen
Winterborn
Alsenz
Münsterappel
Lettweiler
Niedermoschel
Kalkofen
Rehborn
Lettweiler Höhe 380
Spannagel 356
Obermoschel
Alsenz
Oberhausen
Unkenbach
Meisenheim
Oberndorf
Sitters
Gaugrehweiler
Callbach
Schiersfeld
Mannweiler-Cölln
Schmalfelderhof
Hoferhof
Bayerfeld
Steckweiler
Dielkirchen
9
48
50
41
420
428

BINGERBRUCK TO WINTZENHEIM

RECOMMENDED PRODUCERS

Schlossgut Diel
D 55452 Burg Layen
Tel: (06721) 45045
Armin Diel may be best known for his new-oak aged wines from the Pinot family of grapes, but his most exciting wines are the Mosel-like Riesling Spätlesen and Auslesen. Eiswein is an important speciality. Strictly by appointment.

Weingut Michael Schäfer
Hauptstrasse, D 55452 Burg Layen
Tel: (06721) 43097
Well-made Rieslings make up the majority of this reliable estate's wares; also good Scheurebe dessert wines. Appointment recommended.

Weingut Krüger-Rumpf
Rheinstrasse 47
D 55424 Münster-Sarmsheim
Tel: (06721) 43859
The fruity, crisp Rieslings are of dependable high quality. The estate's Weinstube is open from 5pm until midnight; otherwise by appointment.

BINGERBRUCK TO WINTZENHEIM

From Bingerbrück, you can see the vineyards of four wine-growing regions. On the opposite side of the Rhine rises the great mass of the Rüdesheimer Berg in the Rheingau, while on the left bank the last vineyards of the Mittelrhein lie only a few kilometres downstream. In Bingen, on the eastern bank of the Nahe, the vines stand in Rheinhessen, and Bingerbrück's own vineyards are the most northerly in the Nahe region itself.

From Bingerbrück, first take the B9, then the B48 to Münster-Sarmsheim. At first glance, there is nothing particularly remarkable about this town. Enter the imposing tasting room of the Krüger-Rumpf estate, however, and you immediately sense that here is a wine culture that goes a long way back – over two hundred years, in fact. The first-class Dautenpflänzer and Pittersberg vineyards of Münster were planted by Karl Krüger, who founded this estate in 1790. A short distance away lie the no less important Goldlochand Pittermännchen vineyards of Dorsheim in the Trollbachtal. There is a marvellous, if brief, view of these vineyards and the medieval tower of Burg Layen from the A61 Autobahn. The brightly painted signs in the vineyards (by artist Johannes Helle) and the recently restored Burg both belong to the Schlossgut Diel estate. Its owner, polymath Armin

Left *Wide Nahe vineyard terraces, with conventionally trained vines: on wires rather than posts.*

Below *Schlossgut Diel's cellars: its unusual stainless steel tanks were decorated by artist Johannes Helle.*

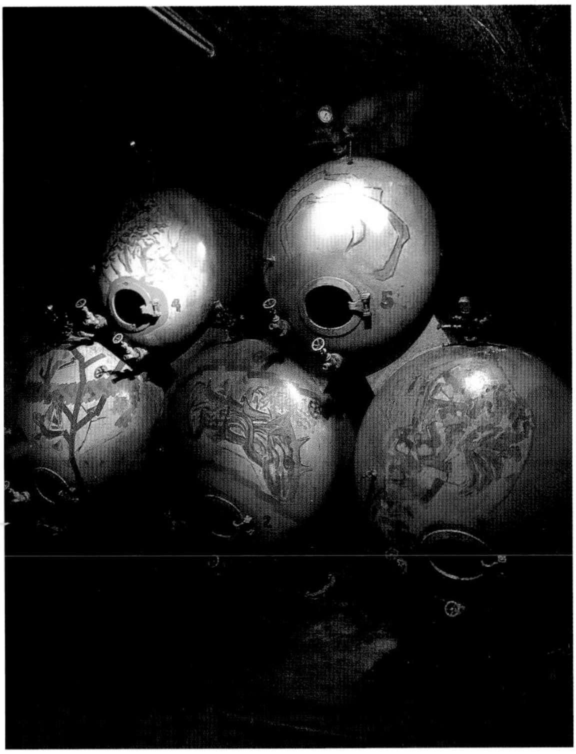

Diel, who is variously a wine journalist, restaurant critic and winemaker, is as important to the region's wine scene as his estate.

The soils on the steep top sites are loamy and close to the surface, with primary rock lying not far below. This results in Rieslings that are packed with fruit, have ample substance and a vibrant acidity which can give them a marvellous brilliance. Their relatively full body means that they can be vinified in either a dry or sweet style. On the heavier soils of the less-steep vineyards, the Pinot family of grapes does well. Weissburgunder (Pinot Blanc), Grauburgunder (Pinot Gris) and Chardonnay all result in good, medium-bodied dry whites, and some increasingly sophisticated Spätburgunder (Pinot Noir) rosé wines are just beginning production.

The towns of Laubenheim and Langenlonsheim have plenty of good vineyards, but neither currently produces wines comparable to those of their immediate neighbours to the north. When the wines here are good, they have an appealing juiciness and a lively but supple acidity; what they usually lack, however, is a little fire and excitement. Some of the great Nahe wines of the past prove that the Rosenheck site of Wintzenheim has the potential to provide more elegant, sophisticated wines.

From here, follow the B48 to Bad Kreuznach.

Weingut Bürgermeister Willi Schweinhardt
Heddesheimer Strasse 1
D 55450 Langenlonsheim
Tel: (06704) 93100
Wilhelm and Axel Schweinhardt make a wide range of substantial fruity wines from more than 30ha of vines.

Weingut Wilhelm Sitzius
Naheweinstrasse 87
D 55450 Langenlonsheim
Tel: (06704) 1309
Rather erratic quality, but some good Rieslings from Langenlonsheim and Niederhausen in the Middle Nahe.

Weingut Tesch
Naheweinstrasse 99
D 55450 Langenlonsheim
Tel: (06704) 93040
Rather coarse, charmless, dry wines, but there are also some good, naturally sweet Riesling Spätlesen and Auslesen.

HOTELS

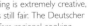

Hotel-Restaurant Trollmühle
Rheinstrasse 199
D 55424 Münster-Sarmsheim
Tel: (06721) 44066
Comfortable hotel close to the A61 Autobahn, but quiet and secluded.

Münsterer Hof
Rheinstrasse 35
D 55424 Münster-Sarmsheim
Tel: 06721 41023
Small country hotel a short walk from the Krüger-Rumpf estate.

Lafer's Stromburg
See restaurants.

RESTAURANTS

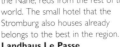

Restaurant Le Val d'Or/Deutscher Michel
in Lafer's Stromburg, Schlossberg 1
D 55442 Stromberg
Tel: (06724) 93100
Austrian chef Johann Lafer runs one of Germany's top restaurants, Le Val d'Or, in this medieval castle in the Hunsrück, 11km from Bingen. The cooking is extremely creative, the prices still fair. The Deutscher Michel offers regional cooking. White wines come exclusively from the Nahe; reds from the rest of the world. The small hotel that the Stromburg also houses already belongs to the best in the region.

Landhaus Le Passe
Naheweinstrasse
D 55559 Bretzenheim
Tel: (0671) 46168
Oliver Szijarto runs this extremely original wine restaurant. The food is a mix of rustic French, Swiss and German cooking.

BAD KREUZNACH

The natural centre of the Nahe region is the spa town of Bad Kreuznach. Although the B48 runs through the town centre, do not underestimate the time it takes to pass through it. The Spa Quarter and the town centre are well worth a stop, however – particularly since Bad Kreuznach is the natural base for anyone wanting to tour the region in style. The best hotels are situated here, and all the Nahe's finest restaurants are within easy striking distance.

Some of the finest vineyards in the Nahe also belong to Bad Kreuznach. The Brückes, Kahlenberg and Krotenpfühl sites all rightly enjoy good reputations, even if the relatively heavy, local soils can make Rieslings a bit ungainly in hot years; average and good vintages give Bad Kreunach's vineyards their best results. The town is home to several important estates, including some of the region's largest, most notably Paul Anheuser and Carl Finkenauer. Sadly, though, it is not easy to find first-class Kreuznach wines at present.

The town's Roman origins are documented by the well-preserved remains of a Roman villa, including a beautiful mosaic preserved in the *Römerhalle* (Roman Hall; note that the fine Restaurant im Gütchen is directly next door). It lies close to the so-called *Neustadt* (New Town), paradoxically now the oldest part of town, with its fine collection of old houses clustered around the *Eiermarkt* (Egg Market). A couple of streets away stands the most famous and, arguably, the most beautiful of these: the Dr Faust Haus. The magician Johannes Faust, about whom the

BAD KREUZNACH

RECOMMENDED PRODUCERS

Weingut Anton Finkenauer
Rheingrafenstrasse 15
D 55543 Bad Kreuznach
Tel: (0671) 62230
Substantial, traditional-style Rieslings, usually with excellent balance. Very good value for money. Appointment recommended.

Weingut Reichsgraf von Plettenberg
Wintzenheimer Strasse
D 55545 Bad Kreuznach
Tel: (0671) 2251
Dependable clean, modern Rieslings. Also good, dry Weissburgunder.

Weingut Carl Finkenauer
Salinenstrasse 60
D 55543 Bad Kreuznach
Tel: (0671) 28771
After some ups and downs, this large estate seems to be back on course. Makes powerful, rich wines that are strong on flavour. Appointment recommended.

Weingut Paul Anheuser
Stromberger Strasse 15–19
D 55545 Bad Kreuznach
Tel: (0671) 28748
Until recently, Bad Kreuznach's number one producer, but pick and choose carefully. The best are full-bodied and expressive.

HOTELS

Steigenberger Avance Kurhaus
Kurhausstrasse 28
D 55543 Bad Kreuznach
Tel: (0671) 8020
Grand and extremely comfortable hotel in the heart of Kreunznach's secluded Spa Quarter.

Insel-Hotel
Kurhausstrasse 10
D 55545 Bad Kreuznach
Tel: (0671) 43043
Less expensive than the Kurhaus, but also well-situated and comfortable.

RESTAURANTS

Restaurant im Gütchen
Hüffelsheimer Strasse 1
D 55545 Bad Kreuznach
Tel: (0671) 42626
Next door to be the Römerhalle and the beautiful Schlosspark, this attractive restaurant could hardly be better situated. Jan Treutle's cooking is at once rustic and sophisticated. An excellent list of Nahe wines.

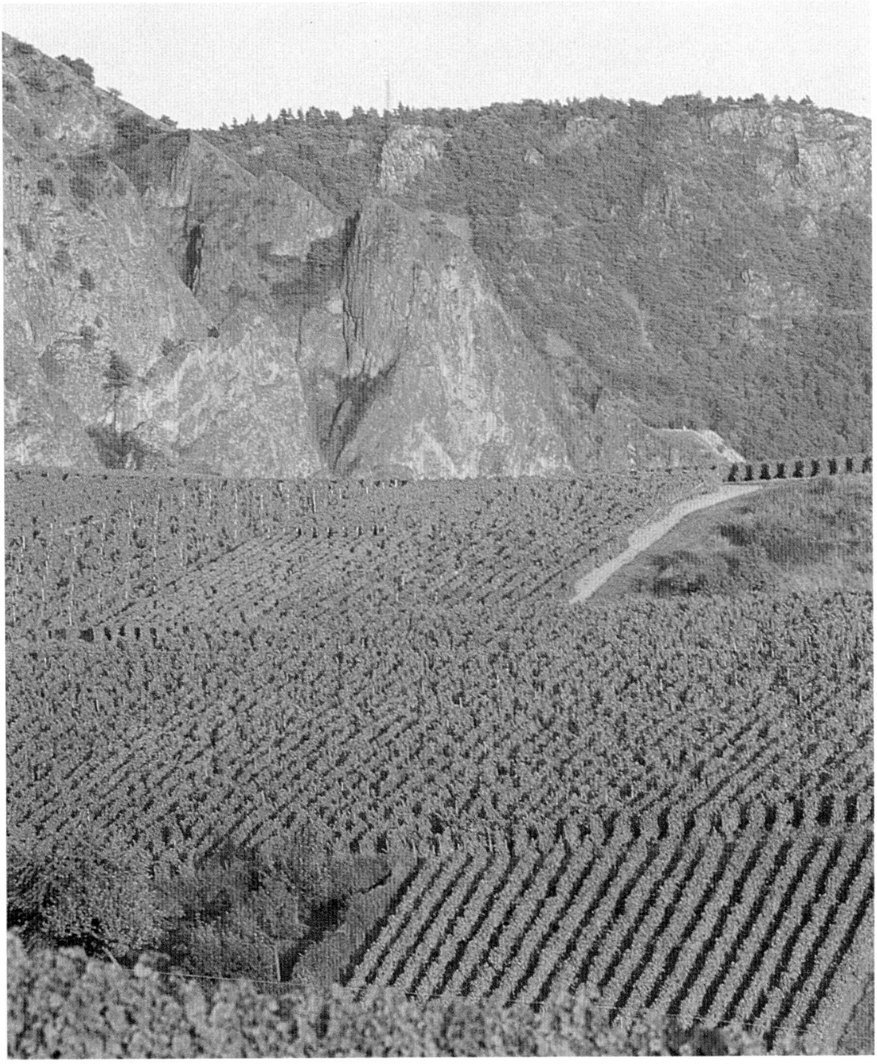

Faust legend is based, is reputed to have lived in this half-timbered house around 1507. From here it is only a short walk to the Alte Nahebrücke, the old Nahe bridge. The bridge dates from 1311, and the row of small houses perching on it date between the 15th and 17th centuries. The bridge leads to the *Kurviertel* (Spa Quarter), with its alleys of old trees and the imposing neo-Baroque Kurhaus. Its dubious claim is to have served as Kaiser Wilhelm II's headquarters during the First World War.

The most picturesque part of the Nahe Valley begins in Bad Kreuznach with the Kurpark (Spa Park). In spite of being very close to the centre of town, the riverside walk, which can be reached by a small bridge next to the Kurhaus, could hardly be more secluded. One of the town's most unusual features is found here: caves where spa guests inhale radon gas, supposedly for health reasons. The clear air of the Middle and Upper Nahe probably has more appeal for wine tourists.

Left and above *Nahe vineyards and wines tend to follow a rule: the more dramatic the scenery, the more complex the wines. Every quality level can be found among them, but whether fine or poor, they are all a reflection of tranquil, unspoilt land.*

Metzler's Gasthof/
Metzler's Weinstube
Hauptstrasse 69
D 55546 Hackenheim
(near Bad Kreuznach)
Tel: (0671) 65312
Just 2km outside Bad Kreuznach. The standard of everything here is very high. Nahe wines dominate the list, next to French and Italian reds. The Weinstube offers simple regional cooking (ask for the full wine list).

Above *The red-roofed town of Bad Münster sheltering under the red Rotenfels cliffs. The thin strip of vineyards that just squeezes between the slope and the town is home to some of the Nahe's top wines.*

FROM BAD MUNSTER TO MONZINGEN

RECOMMENDED PRODUCERS

Weingut H Dönnhoff
Bahnhofstrasse 11
D 55585 Oberhausen
Tel: (06755) 263
From extensive holdings in the best vineyards of Niederhausen, Schlossböckelheim and Oberhausen. Helmut Dönnhoff makes Rieslings of the greatest sophistication and individuality. Many of the top wines sell out very quickly.
Strictly by appointment.

Weingut Emrich Schönleber
Naheweinstrasse 10a
D 55569 Monzingen
Tel: (06751) 2733
Far and away the leading producer of the Upper Nahe, Werner Schönleber makes Rieslings that are at once charming and full of minerally character. Friendly prices.
Appointment recommended.

BAD MUNSTER TO MONZINGEN

Close to Bad Münster, the gigantic, red, porphyry mass of the Rotenfels cliffs towers 200 metres above the surrounding countryside, announcing the beginnings of the great vineyards of the Middle Nahe. Take the B48 out of Bad Kreuznach to Bad Münster, then follow the signs for Norheim and Niederhausen. The road runs directly between the foot of the Rotenfels and the river, alongside the narrow strip of vines that clings to screes. This is the Rotenfels, where the famous Traiser Bastei vineyard is situated. Less than two kilometres along the road in Norheim is the turning for Traisen, home of the Bastei's champion, Dr Peter Crusius' estate. If you have time, and do not suffer from vertigo, ask in Traisen for directions to the peak of the Rotenfels. The views are sensational.

Norheim is an unremarkable little town that boasts some rather remarkable vineyards. The finest of these is the precipitous, terraced Dellchen (though the Kafels and Kirscheck are also first class). The Norheim vineyards lead directly to the famous sites of Niederhausen. After the road crosses the railway line just before the village of Niederhausen, the view of the vineyards is obscured; however, the forested slopes on the other bank of the Nahe more than compensate for this. For an improved view of the vineyards, take the small turning back under the railway line signposted Niederhausen. Here there are several good small estates, of which Oskar Mathern is the best and Jakob Schneider the best-known.

Both Niederhausen and neighbouring Schlossböckelheim were made famous by the Nahe State Domaine, situated between the two villages and surrounded by the region's finest and most magnificent vineyards. You could argue long and hard about which is the greatest, although history says the Niederhäuser Hermannshöhle is number one. The Prussian vineyard classification published on a map in 1901 (recently reprinted by the Nahe VDP) rated this site first among the Nahe vineyards, though at this time the famous Niederhäuser Hermannsberg and Schlossböckelheimer Felsenberg vineyards had not yet been planted.

The Rieslings from these vineyards express the qualities that make the area's wine among Germany's greatest: tremendous intensity and expression combined with great delicacy and elegance. Today, the Dönnhoff estate in Oberhausen, just across the Luitpoldbrücke on the other bank of the river, makes the best wines from these slopes. Thankfully, the State Domaine is finally emerging from a lengthy crisis.

The fine vineyards do not stop here, however. From Oberhausen, continue to Sobernheim, then follow the signs for Monzingen. Not only does the centre of Monzingen have some of the most beautiful Gothic and half-timbered buildings, its Frühlingsplätzchen and Halenberg sites also foster some excellent Rieslings. The wines are slightly less dramatic and aromatic, but are full of character and can achieve considerable sophistication in the hands of producers such as Emrich Schönleber. From here, the B41 continues up the Nahe to Kirn and Idar-Oberstein. In the other direction it provides the quickest route back to Bad Kreuznach.

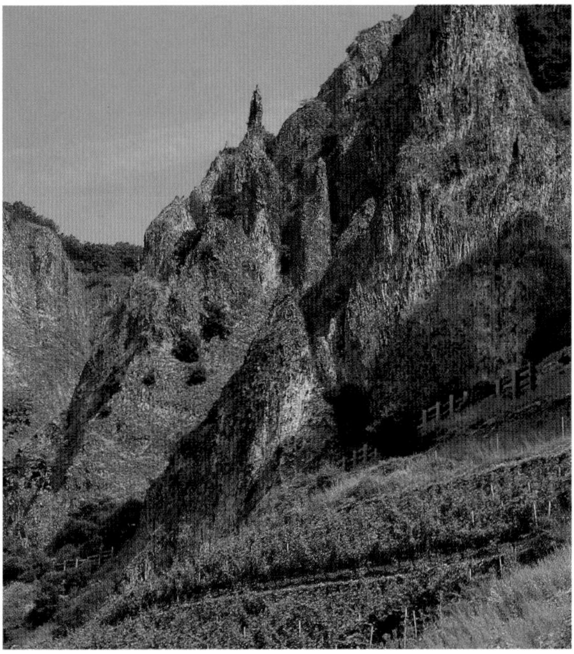

Weingut Crusius
Hauptstrasse 2
D 55595 Traisen
Tel: (0671) 33953
After a shaky period, this established star of the region is back on form. Extremely clean, expressive dry and naturally sweet Rieslings. The Traiser Bastei sell out fast. By appointment only.

Weingut Oskar Mathern
Winzerstrasse 7
D 55585 Niederhausen
Tel: (06758) 6714
Young Helmut Mathern is the up-and-coming name of the Middle Nahe, making Niederhausen Rieslings with elegance and structure. Very good value for money. By appointment only.

Weingut Hehner-Kiltz
Hauptstrasse 4
D 55596 Waldböckelheim
Tel: (06758) 7918
Rather variable quality, but the best Rieslings from the top sites of Schlossböckelheim are often impressive. The Hehners' wine restaurant offers good regional cooking based on products from local farms. Good river fish and game. Appointment recommended for wine tastings.

RESTAURANTS

See Hehner Kilz.

PLACES OF INTEREST

Idar-Oberstein
The twin town of Idar-Obsterin, 50km upstream from Bad Kreuznach, nestles among the first hills of the Hunsrück. The 15th-century Felsenkirche, built into the side of a cliff, is just a short walk from the centre of Oberstein. The town itself is the centre of the country's gem-mining industry, and its gem and precious stone museum is well worth a visit – even if it is housed in an ugly tower block.

Left *The Traiser Bastei vineyard – from where the best of the Rotenfels wines come.*

THE OUTLYING VALLEYS

By no means do all of the region's best wines come from vineyards close to the Nahe River. Many very good vineyards are found in the tributary valleys of the Nahe, surrounded by beautiful countryside. One of the least-spoiled sections of the region is Wallhausen in the Gräfenbach Valley, home to Germany's oldest wine estate, Prinz zu Salm-Dalberg. The estate's label depicts the Dalburg fortress, which is today a mighty ruin a few kilometres further up the valley, close to Dalberg. Today the estate is housed in the not-much-less-imposing Schloss of Wallhausen. Apart from the odd satellite antennae, everything looks much as it must have centuries ago. The Rieslings from Wallhausen's Johannisberg site possess a piercing, racy acidity. A short distance away lies Roxheim, its famous Berg vineyard producing silkier, more elegant wines. These first-class sites deserve to be better known.

On the other side of Bad Kreuznach lies the most important of the outlying valleys of the region, that of the Alsenz. It is easily reached by taking the B48 from Bad Kreuznach, which follows its entire course south (in the direction of Rockenhausen). At the beginning of the Alsenz Valley stands the Ebernburg castle, which dates back to at least 1209 – though what one sees today is from later centuries. From here it is only a few kilometres to Altenbamberg, where the State Domain's vineyard has made some excellent wines. Dessert wine specialist Adolf Lotzbeyer, in Feilbingert, is also worth a visit.

Right *The colourful Schloss Wallhausen: home of the Prinz zu Salm estate – the oldest in Germany.*

THE OUTLYING VALLEYS

RECOMMENDED PRODUCERS

Weingut Adolf Lotzbeyer
Kirchstrasse 6
D 67824 Feilbingert
Tel: (06708) 2287
Makes superb dessert wines from Riesling (particularly those from the first-class Norheimer Dellchen) and Scheurebe. The other wines are generally good, if unspectacular. Appointment recommended.

Weingut Schmidt
Luitpoldstrasse 24
D 67823 Obermoschel
Tel: (06362) 1265
Very consistent producer of fruity Rieslings; the Spätlesen and Auslesen have a sometimes impressive natural sweetness. Very good value for money. Appointment recommended.

Weingut Hahnmühle
Alsenzstrasse 25
SD 67822 Mannweiler-Cölln
Tel: (06362) 2693
Organic winemakers Peter and Martina Linxweiler specialize in dry Rieslings and Traminers. These are uncompromising wines: always minerally, but sometimes also austere. Appointment recommended.

Weingut Prinz zu Salm-Dalberg
Im Schloss
D 55595 Wallhausen
Tel: (06706) 944411
Michael Prinz zu Salm-Salm, president of the VDP, concentrates on light, racy Rieslings, but he also makes good Spätburgunder rosés. Appointment recommended; closed weekends.

Ten kilometres along the valley just before the town of Alsenz is the turning for Obermoschel (B420), where the valley's largest estate, Schmidt, is based. Here the soils of the best sites are slate, and the Rieslings taste like larger-scale Mosel wines. The best producers are the Hahnmühle estate of Cölln, which is housed in a medieval mill, and the region's most southern estate, Steitz of Dellkirchen. The peak of the almost 700-metre-high Donnersberg towers above the surrounding hills. It is worth driving to the top if the weather is good for the panoramic views over the Nahe region and neighbouring Rheinhessen. You can pick up the A63 motorway to Mainz virtually at the foot of the Donnersberg.

Below *The steep Rotenfels cliffs: climb to the top, if you have the energy, and you'll be met with sensational views*

The Rheingau

Although the Rheingau's wines are no longer the world's most expensive or glamorous as they were a century ago, this region remains the most famous of all Germany's 13 wine-growing areas. Its sweeping hillside vineyards are the birthplace of the fine German wines we know today. Great Rheingau Rieslings match power with elegance. As young wines, they are less exuberant and firmer than Mosel or Nahe Rieslings; with age they acquire a grace and aromatic refinement that is unique.

The landscape and climate of the Rheingau are both different from those of Germany's other wine-growing regions for several reasons. For a start, this is the only section of the Rhine's northwards course where the river flows from east to west. The hillsides on its right bank are therefore generally south-facing and are sheltered from the northerly winds by the Taunus Mountains, which once formed an effective barrier against invading armies, making the Rheingau virtually an island – a fact, some argue, that shapes the mentality of some inhabitants today. Certainly, a streak of pride can be encountered here, and a self-confidence that German winegrowers elsewhere rarely show.

Close to the river, the vineyards are generally planted on the slopes of gently rolling hills. The vines give the scenery an appealing gentleness, and they benefit greatly from the heat reservoir of the Rhine's waters. Higher up towards the Taunus forest, the landscape becomes more dramatic as the slopes become steeper. The air is considerably cooler here, but the well-exposed inclines concentrate the sun's rays; thus, in spite of lying on the 50th parallel, the region's best vineyards are climatically favoured. Extremes of heat and cold are rare.

Unlike the Mosel, where the vineyards tower over the architecture, the Rheingau's vineyards are punctuated by a series of imposing castles, monasteries, palaces and

Above and left *Schloss Johannisberg, one of the finest monuments to German wine culture: its first vines were established around 800AD; from then on its history is of racy, elegant and stylish Rheingau wines.*

There is a fascinating variety of architectural landmarks in the Rheingau: Geisenheim's Schloss Schönborn (below) *and Assmannshausen's church* (bottom) *illustrate two of the different styles.*

churches that dominate the landscape. To quote Goethe, in the Rheingau, *Johannisberg thront über alles* – the Johannisberg castle reigns over everything, as if it were seated on a throne. The Rheingau's architectural richness bears witness to the power and wealth of the church here from the Middle Ages until the secularization of 1803, and the increasing role played by the aristocracy during 17th to 19th centuries. The clerical and aristocratic estates made the Rheingau famous, and their names are inextricably linked to it.

If the Rheingau's aura is less bright than it once was, it is because many of its great estates have not kept up the high standards of the past, and a group of smaller, family-owned estates have overtaken them. The Charta Estates Association was founded in 1984 to promote the region's dry wines and win back its former glory. Together with the region's association of quality producers, the *Verband Deutscher Prädikats- und Qualitätsweingüter* (VDP), and the Rheingau Winegrowers Association, they have recently conducted an intensive campaign to establish Germany's first vineyard classification. With the expected approval of Hessen's state parliament, 1997 vintage wines from classified sites will be entitled to the designation *Erstes Gewächs*, meaning first growth, similar to France's *appellation contrôlée*.

Another positive development in the region is the extraordinary growth in the Rheingau's gastronomic and hotel industry. Only Baden can offer a comparable selection of top restaurants and fine hotels. The fact that they and the region's leading wine estates are concentrated within a stretch of country little more than 30 kilometres

Rheingau

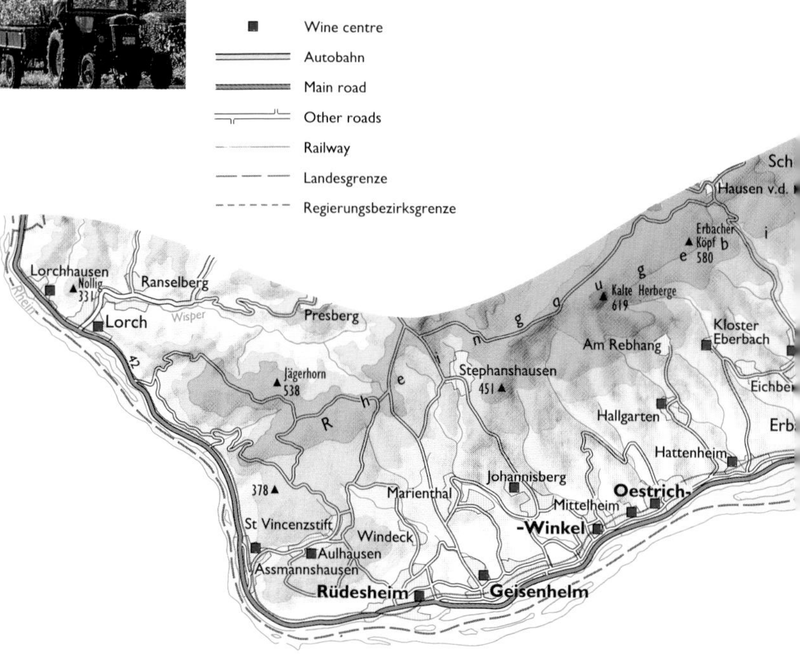

wide makes this a very popular destination for wine tourists in Germany. The proximity of the Frankfurt-Wiesbaden-Mainz conurbation also means that there are numerous day-trippers during fine weather; in the summer, you are advised to make reservations early.

Below *Colourful decorated and timbered Rheingau buildings. It is not just castles, churches, monasteries and palaces that decorate the scene here, almost every street reflects pride in its architecture and appearance.*

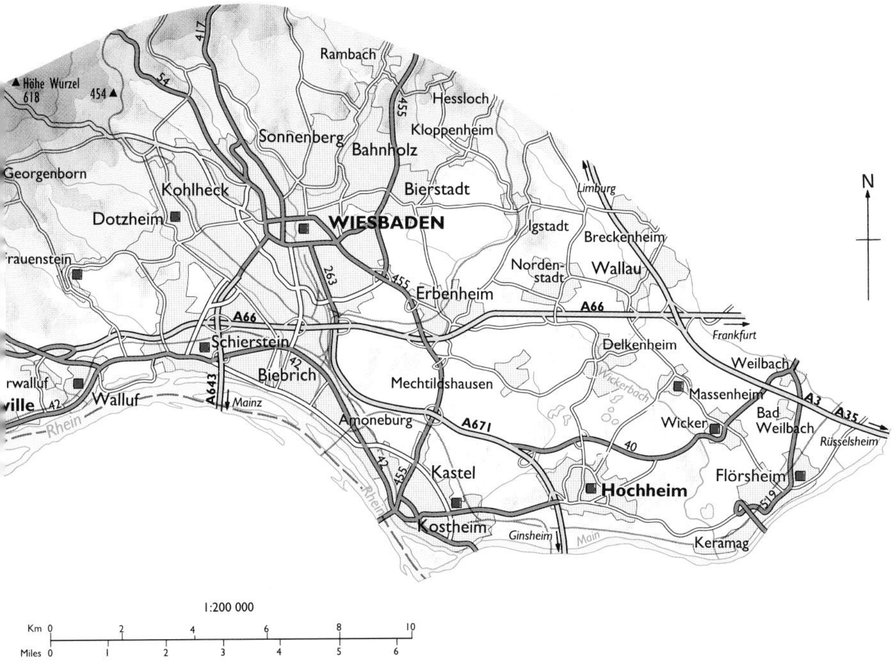

Above *All the defense needed here at Lorch am Rhein has been provided by its steep Riesling vineyards and the river beneath it.*
Above right *Assmannshausen: the local winemakers argue that its vineyards will achieve success only with the black Spätburgunder grape.*

LORCH AM RHEIN

The western extremity of the Rheingau is the only part of the region that lies within the Rhine Gorge, rather than in the broader section of the valley where the river flows from east to west. The landscape, climate, soils and character of the local Riesling wines all resemble those of the Mittelrhein, on the opposite bank of the river. Approaching the region from Koblenz along the B42, this is the first point reached in the Rheingau.

The sleek, steely Rieslings from the vineyards of Lorch am Rhein and Lorchhausen, at the northern extremity of the Rheingau, could easily be mistaken for Mittelrhein wines. However, Lorch itself is very different from the towns on the opposite bank. Here there are no town walls or other fortifications, and the river saved the buildings from much of the destruction during the wars of the 17th century. The magnificent Hilchenhaus, owned by the Graf von Kanitz estate, is the finest Renaissance building on this stretch of the river, and its red-and-white gabled façade dominates the face the town presents to the river. From Lorch, the valley of the Rhine's tributary, the Wisp, runs up into the Taunus Mountains. Its course leads through some of the most beautiful country around. Given limited time, this is the best way to get to know the hilly landscape. Otherwise, take the B42 to Assmannshausen.

LORCH AM RHEIN

RECOMMENDED PRODUCERS

Weingut Graf von Kanitz
Rheinstrasse 49
D 65391 Lorch am Rhein
Tel: (06726) 346
The Rheingau's largest organic wine producer, specializing in sleek, dry Rieslings. Appointment recommended. The estate's wine restaurant is located in the Hilchenhaus, and is open every day except Thursday from noon to 11pm.

Weingut Troitzsch (Haus Schöneck)
Bächergrund 12
D 65391 Lorch am Rhein
Tel: (06726) 9481
Bone-dry Rieslings and good, dry Scheureben are the focus of the Pusinellis here. By appointment only.

RESTAURANTS

Hilchenhaus
See recommended producers.

ASSMANNSHAUSEN

Assmannshausen is the Rheingau's only wine community specializing in red wine. As in the Ahr region, this is primarily the result of historical accident. The local

vintner's argument that the slate soil of the villages' spectacularly steep vineyards is predestined for Pinot Noir will not convince anyone who knows either the great Pinot Noirs from the limestone marl soils of the Côte d'Or, or the magnificent Rieslings from the slate soils of the Mosel. However, try a glass of good Assmannshausen Spätburgunder with a plate of roast game in the Hotel Krone's famous dining room, and the argument, whether for or against, seems irrelevant. The best Assmannshausen reds may be expensive, but they are all full of intense, red, berry fruit and elegant tannins. In the picturesque surroundings of Assmannshausen, they taste even better.

The Krone is not one of the Rheingau's finest hotels; rather it is a monument to the region's glorious history. It is worth staying or eating here just so you can study the hotel's collection of photographs and paintings dating from the late-19th and early-20th centuries. They bring the Rheingau's golden age to life in a way books cannot. Today, most visitors to Assmannshausen, if not to the Krone, come by bus or by the two chairlifts that span the Niederwald to Rüdesheim. The majority of Assmannshausen's red wines are still made in a pink, sweetish style for these tourists, and are therefore best avoided.

Left *The neatly cultivated Hollenberg vineyard at Assmannshausen – here too the speciality is red grapes.*

ASSMANNSHAUSEN

RECOMMENDED PRODUCERS

Weingut August Kesseler
Lorcher Strasse 16
D 65385 Assmannshausen
Tel: (06722) 2513
International-style red wines with a gentle touch of new oak. The intensely fruity rosés and Rieslings are also very good. No bargains here. Strictly by appointment.

Staatsweingut Assmannshausen
Höllenbergstrasse 10
D 65385 Assmannshausen
Tel: (06722) 2273
Well-made Spätburgunder red wines without new oak. Also impressive rosé dessert wines. Closed at weekends.

Weingut Robert König
D 65385 Assmannshausen
Tel: (06722) 1064
Young Robert König has breathed new life in to this specialist producer of Spätburgunder reds and rosés. The nearest thing to good value for money in Assmannshausen. By appointment only.

HOTELS

Hotel Krone
Rheinuferstrasse 10
D 65385 Assmannshausen
Tel: (06722) 4030
Luxurious hotel, the oldest part of which date back to the 16th century. The rooms are masterpieces of Wilhelmine interior design, the restaurant likewise unashamedly old-fashioned (look for game). The amazing list of Rheingau and Bordeaux wines includes many older vintages at friendly prices. If you can't afford to stay, at least drink a glass of wine under the wisteria-covered pergola and admire the view of the Rhine. During the last few years, the hotel's own wine estate has made ever-better reds.

Alte Bauernschänke-Nassauer Hof
Niederwaldstrasse 23
D 65385 Assmannshausen
Tel: (06722) 2332
Comfortable hotel situated in a half-timbered house which dates back to 1408.

RESTAURANTS

Hotel Krone See hotels.

Above *Of the variety of sites to see in Rüdesheim, the views from the River Rhine are some of the finest.*
Below right *The town of Rüdesheim itself has a great deal to look at: there are few themes and many contrasts – imposing Rheingau buildings always present.*

RUDESHEIM

The great Riesling vineyards of the Rheingau begin where the Rhine turns north between Rüdesheim and Assmannshausen. This is the famous Rüdesheimer Berg, divided into the Berg Schlossberg, Berg Rottland and Berg Roseneck sites, the only steep vineyards in the region that standing directly next to the river. The massive terraces of vines provide the most imposing sight in the entire region (and are best seen from the ferry connecting Rüdesheim with Bingen). The wines produced from them are hardly less impressive, although their strength lies in their silkiness and the manner in which they marry great intensity with inner equilibrium. This applies as much to dry wines with 13° natural alcohol as to the greatest Trockenbeerenauslesen.

Rüdesheim itself is a town full of contradictions. On the one hand, there are magnificent historical monuments ranging from the 12th-century Brömserburg castle which houses the town's wine museum, to the enormous Niederwald *Denkmal* (monument) commemorating the German victory in the Franco-Prussian war of 1870–71, which stands above the town. On the other hand, there is the Drosselgasse, an alley packed with tourists and tacky souvenir shops along the bank of the Rhine. The contrast between this atmosphere and the tasting rooms of the best estates could hardly be more dramatic. The Georg Breuer

Rheingau: Rüdesheim

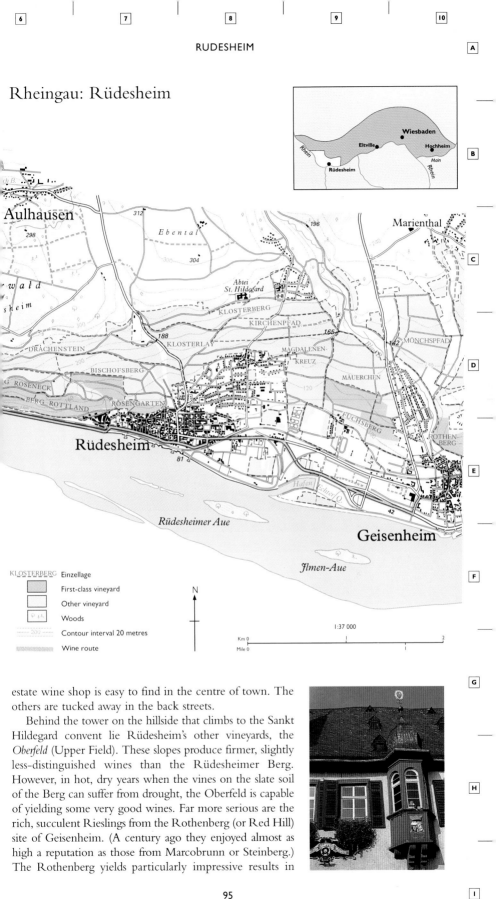

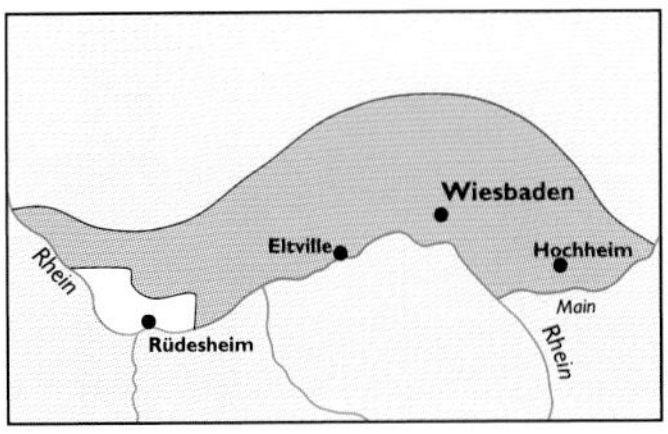

estate wine shop is easy to find in the centre of town. The others are tucked away in the back streets.

Behind the tower on the hillside that climbs to the Sankt Hildegard convent lie Rüdesheim's other vineyards, the *Oberfeld* (Upper Field). These slopes produce firmer, slightly less-distinguished wines than the Rüdesheimer Berg. However, in hot, dry years when the vines on the slate soil of the Berg can suffer from drought, the Oberfeld is capable of yielding some very good wines. Far more serious are the rich, succulent Rieslings from the Rothenberg (or Red Hill) site of Geisenheim. (A century ago they enjoyed almost as high a reputation as those from Marcobrunn or Steinberg.) The Rothenberg yields particularly impressive results in

RUDESHEIM

RECOMMENDED PRODUCERS

Weingut Josef Leitz
Theodor-Heuss-Strasse 5
D 65385 Rüdesheim
Tel: (06722) 2293
Johannes Leitz makes some of the most sophisticated Rieslings in the Rheingau. Excellent quality, both in the dry and naturally sweet styles. From November to March, 4pm to midnight, the wines can be drunk at the estate's eccentric wine bar, zur Hufschmied (Schmittstrasse 6). Otherwise, visits are strictly by appointment.

Weingut Georg Breuer
Grabenstrasse 8
D 65385 Rüdesheim
Tel: (06722) 1027
Bernhard Breuer is not only one of the most dynamic figures in the Rheingau, he is also one of its leading quality wine producers. The dry Rieslings of recent vintages have been first class, but the dessert wines are a little more erratic. The wine shop is open Monday to Saturday for tastings during regular shop hours.

Weingut Dr Heinrich Nägler
Friedrichstrasse 22
D 65385 Rüdesheim
Tel: (06722) 2835
A well-known estate with some good wines from the Rüdesheimer Berg. Appointment recommended; closed Sunday.

HOTELS

Jagdschloss Niederwald
D 65385 Rüdesheim
Tel: (06722) 1004
This comfortable hotel is situated 5km north of Rüdesheim in the Niederwald forest. It has a swimming pool, tennis courts and sauna.

Rüdesheimer Schloss
See restaurants.

Central Hotel
Kirchstrasse 6
D 65385 Rüdesheim
Tel: (06722) 3036
As the name suggests, this is a centrally located hotel. Comfortable and moderately priced, with fewer noise problems than most in the centre of Rüdesheim.

RESTAURANTS

Bistro Berg Schlossberg
Grabenstrasse 8
D 65385 Rüdesheim
Tel: (06722) 1026
New bistro with tasty modern cooking. A fine list of wines from the Georg Breuer estate, among others.

cooler, wetter years. The Kläuserweg site next door produces firmer, more assertive wines, and needs a warm summer in order to give its best.

GEISENHEIM

Today, Geisenheim is best known for its wine school and research station, founded in 1872 and situated at the foot of the Rothenberg. To reach it, follow the B42 to Geisenheim, taking the turning for the town centre, then ask for directions. Sadly, the town does not have any important wine estates, and the best Geisenheim wines are actually made elsewhere (Johannishof, Geheimrat J Wegeler). In the old centre of Geisenheim, you will find the 16th-century Schönborner Hof and the medieval *Heiligenkreuzkirche* (Church of the Holy Cross) with its massive 19th-century twin towers that earned it the nickname 'the cathedral of the Rheingau'. Drive on to the eastern edge of town (past some light industrial works) and take the turning for Johannisberg.

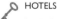

Rüdesheimer Schloss
Steingasse 10
D 65385 Rüdesheim
Tel: (06722) 90500
A new, small hotel situated in an 18th-century house with stylish, modern rooms. The restaurant has been substantially renovated, the regional cooking has gained in sophistication, and the astonishing list of Rheingau wines (going back to the 19th century!) is still expanding. What has not changed is the crowds of tourists and the oompah music.

GEISENHEIM

RECOMMENDED PRODUCERS

Forschungsanstalt Geisenheim
Kirchspiel
D 65366 Geisenheim
Tel: (06722) 502171
Good Rieslings, particularly from the Geisenheimer Rothenberg. Appointment recommended; closed weekends.

RESTAURANTS

Schlossweinstube Kosakenberg
Bahnstrasse 1
D 65366 Geisenheim
Tel: (06722) 71543
Attractive wine bar of the von Zwierlein estate, positioned close to Geisenheim's railway station. Simple fare, rustic wines and a good atmosphere.

Harvest time at Rüdesheim's Berg Rottland vineyard (top), *and autumn approaching at the Bischofsberg and Rosengarten sites* (left)*: these are home to some serious Rieslings – some of the best of which come from the George Breuer estate* (above) *and are matured in oak (though not all the barrels will be as ornate as this one).*

JOHANNISBERG AND VOLLRADS

The view of Schloss Johannisberg from the bank of the Rhine just outside Geisenheim (B42) is one of the most magnificent in Germany. Schloss Johannisberg is not only one of the most beautiful buildings in Germany's winegrowing regions, it is also an outstanding monument of German wine culture. Legend has it that the first vines were planted here on the order of Charlemagne who, from his winter palace in Ingelheim on the opposite bank of the Rhine, noticed that the winter snow melted here first. A document dated 817 and bearing the seal of his son Ludwig the Pious seems to confirm this fact. The Benedictine abbey of Johannisberg was founded around 1100; its chapel dates from shortly thereafter. The façade seen today dates from the early 18th century, and the beautiful barrel cellar dates from 1720, shortly after the estate came to be owned by the Bishop of Fulda. A climb to the Schloss should not be missed for its architectural splendour, the view and the excellent wine restaurant.

Here, the first recorded Riesling monoculture was planted in 1720 (previously all vineyard plantings were

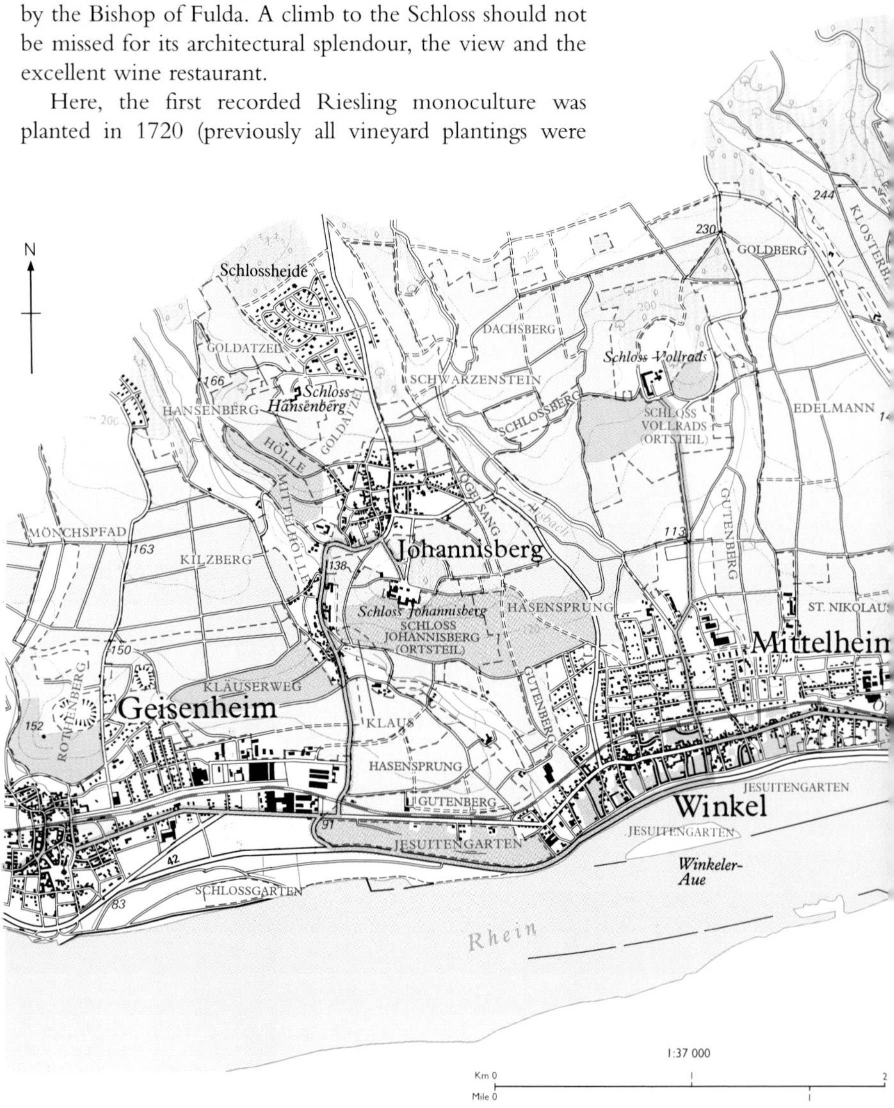

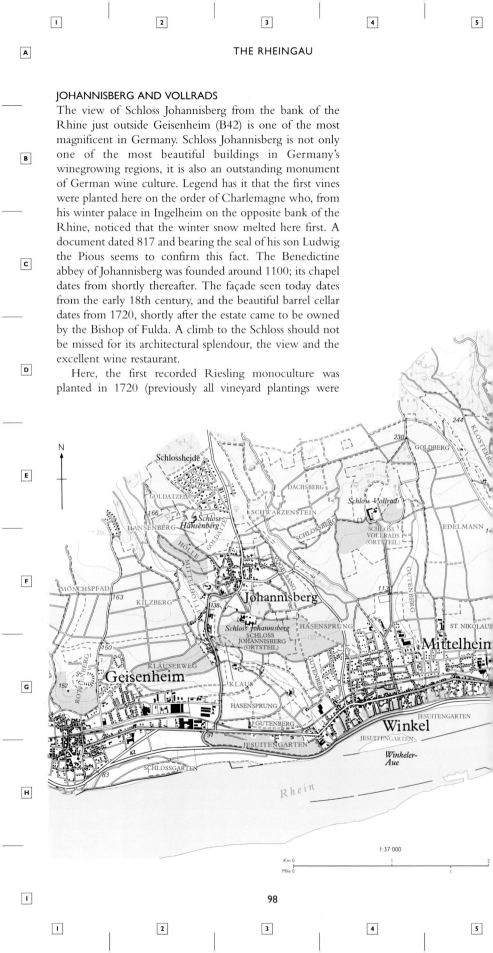

Central Rheingau: West

KLOSTERBERG Einzellage

First-class vineyard

Other vineyard

Woods

Contour interval 20 metres

Wine route

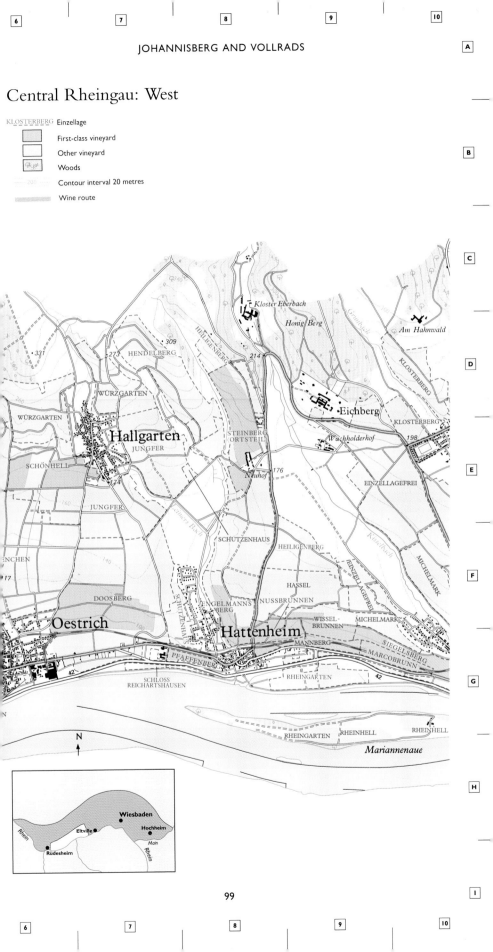

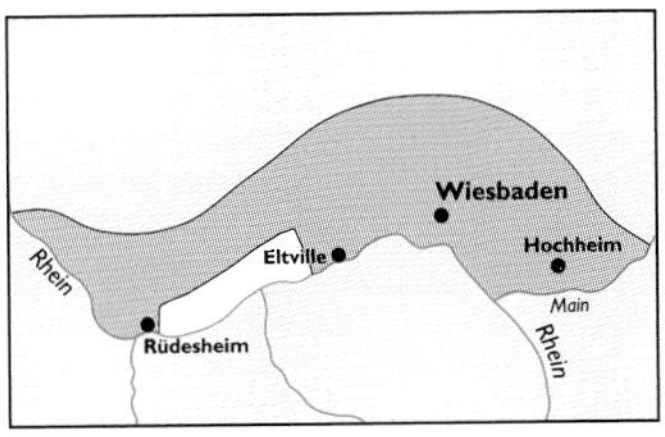

JOHANNISBERG AND VOLLRADS

RECOMMENDED PRODUCERS

Fürst von Metternich-Winneburg'sche Domäne Schloss Johannisberg & G H von Mumm
D 65366 Johannisberg
Tel: (06722) 70090
These two famous estates share the same cellars and administration, but their wines differ considerably. The Schloss Johannisberg wines are the better (and more expensive) of the two, but you still need to pick and choose; the von Mumm wines can be poor. The wine shop is open Monday to Friday and Saturday mornings. Tours by appointment only.

Above *It was here at Schloss Johannisberg that Riesling was first cultivated on its own – and with marvellous results, including the discovery of beneficial Edelfäule.*
Right *The vineyards of Schloss Vollrads – reminiscent of Bordeaux.*

Gemischter Satz, or a mix of vine varieties), and soon afterwards the bottling of the estate's best wines began. This enabled the real greatness of Riesling, which can only be achieved through ageing in the bottle, to be realized.

In 1775, the messenger bearing the Bishop's order that the harvest should begin was delayed, so by the time word did arrive, all the grapes were rotten. Happily, the rot was

Edelfäule, or noble rot, and the result was the first Spätlese wines. The enormous success of these led Schloss Johannisberg to systematize late harvesting and to develop the selective picking necessary to produce the first Auslese, BA and TBA wines in subsequent years.

What makes Johannisberg's wines so remarkable is their racy elegance – apparent even at the highest levels of concentration. In a poor vintage, this can make them a little hard in their youth, but in good years they can have a breathtaking brilliance. Apart from the great hillside of the Schloss, the best vineyards are the Hölle/Mittelhölle and the Klaus. The leading producer today is clearly the Johannishof estate, located at the foot of the Johannisberg itself (on the main road).

Only one-and-a-half kilometres from Johannisberg lies the almost equally famous estate of Schloss Vollrads. Here, the estate and vineyard names are identical, and Vollrads presents a completely different face to Johannisberg. Its moated tower of 1330 is the oldest part of the complex, to which the Baroque palace around it was added in the late-17th century. The estate has always enjoyed a high reputation for its Auslese, BA and TBA wines, and it is well-recognized that the steely, regular-quality wines need time to show their best. Just as at Schloss Johannisberg, the architecture and the estate's wine restaurant alone are worth the journey.

Weingut Johannishof/H H Eser
Im Grund 63, D 65366 Johannisberg
Tel: (06722) 8216
Young Johannes Eser makes the finest Joahnnisberg wines today. Also excellent Charta wines and Spätlesen. Appointment recommended; essential Saturdays; closed Sundays.

Weingut Prinz von Hessen
Grund 1, D 65366 Johannisberg
Tel: (06722) 8172
Large estate making poor, dry wines, but some fine Auslesen and higher Prädikat dessert wines. Appointment recommended. Closed weekends.

Weingut Schloss Vollrads and Fürst Löwenstein
D 65375 Winkel
Tel: (06723) 660
After a period of serious under-performance, Vollrads is doing somewhat better again. Generally makes rather simple, dry wines with plenty of acidity. Appointment recommended.

RESTAURANTS

Gutsschänke Schloss Johannisberg
D 65366 Johannisberg
Tel: (06722) 8538
Excellent regional cooking with a modern touch (plus good French cheese) from Dieter Biesler, and a list of wines from the estate.

Gutsrestaurant Schloss Vollrads
D 65375 Winkel
Tel: (06723) 5270
Members of the team from the Michelin-star Graues Haus restaurant prepare a reinterpretation of the region's cooking, which is rather hit and miss. Wines include those from Schloss Vollrads and Fürst Löwenstein.

Top left *Schloss Johannisberg: the statue commemorates the messenger who luckily delayed 1775's harvest.*
Above *The tower at Schloss Vollrads is one of its oldest features.*

OESTRICH-WINKEL

The ancient town of Winkel boasts some of the Rheingau's oldest buildings. Approaching it along the B42 from the west leads past the main slope of the first-class Jesuitengarten site, then by the Graues Haus, and a short distance further, the Romanesque basilica of Saint Agidius. The *Graues Haus* (literally, 'Grey House') is almost certainly the oldest stone house in Germany. It was the residence of the Knights of Greiffenclau from 1050 to 1330, when they moved to Schloss Vollrads (technically, however, it still remains in their ownership). It now houses the region's finest restaurant, which has been sensitively integrated into the ancient building. The Brentano Haus (Lindenplatz 2), home of the Baron von Brentano estate, stands out among the many fine, old houses in the town centre. The Brentanos were close friends of Goethe, and several rooms have been preserved as they were during the time of Goethe's visit in 1814. Today, the Brentanos regularly hold literary and musical evenings in these rooms (for reservations, tel: 06723 2068).

Oestrich, Mittelheim and Winkel effectively form a single town. It is worth taking the B42 from one to the other in order to see the 16th-century crane on the river bank at Oestrich, once used for loading barrels of wine onto river boats. As well as the fine Gothic church of Saint Martin (completed in 1508), Oestrich has a clutch of

Wine in the Rheingau was once transported by river to its market place: the crane at Oestrich (right) *– built in the 1500s – was used to load the barrels onto boats.*

OESTRICH-WINKEL

RECOMMENDED PRODUCERS

Weingüter Geheimrat J Wegeler Erben
Friedensplatz 9
D 65375 Oestrich-Winkel
Tel: (06723) 7031
Deinhard's Rheingau estate is one of the region's largest and one of its most important quality producers. Director Norbert Holderrieth concentrates on dry Rieslings; the Charta wines and Geheimrat J brand are particularly impressive. There are also some very good dessert wines. Strictly by appointment.

Weingut August Eser
Friedensplatz 19
D 65375 Oestrich
Tel: (06723) 5032
Garrulous Joachim Eser makes a wide range of dry and naturally sweet Rieslings – rich, juicy wines that offer good value for money. Appointment recommended; closed Sunday.

Weingut Peter Jakob Kühn
Mühlstrasse 70
D 65375 Oestrich
Tel: (06723) 2299
During the last five years, newcomer Peter Kühn has attracted a lot of attention with his extremely clean, appealingly fruity, dry and dessert Rieslings. By appointment only.

Weingut Wilfried Querbach
Dr-Rody-Strasse 2
D 65375 Oestrich
Tel: (06723) 3887
Small estate with slightly erratic wines. Charta and Spätlese Trockens are generally the most expressive, and good value. Appointment recommended; essential at weekends.

Hupfeld & Königin Victoria Berg
Rheingaustrasse 113
D 65375 Mittelheim
Tel: (06723) 3307
The 5ha monopoly Königin-Victoria-Berg vineyard in Hochheim produces this estate's best and most substantial wines. The rest are a mixed bag, often simple. By appointment only; closed Sunday.

elegant estates. In the centre of town, the J Wegeler (Deinhard) and August Eser estates lie just yards apart. Although they are the leading producers of Oestrich wines, both have significant holdings in other parts of the region. In the back streets, you will find the good Peter Jakob Kühn and Wilfried Querbach estates.

Oestrich's finest Rieslings come from the best parts of the Doosberg and Lenchen sites, both of which were greatly expanded under the 1971 wine law. The vineyards' deep soils yield substantial wines, which are stronger on richness than subtlety. The comparison with Winkel's best wines is a natural one, since they, too, have plenty of body and structure. However, the more piquant acidity of the wines from the Hasensprung and Jesuitengarten sites of Winkel allow them to develop more elegance with ageing in the bottle. The lesser wines of both Winkel and Oestrich can be very tart; thankfully, a good proportion is sold in bulk for sparkling-wine production.

Above *Graues Haus in Winkel – one of the region's best restaurants, boasting a wine list that reaches as far back as 1921.*

HOTELS

Hotel Schwann
Rheinallee 5
D 65375 Oestrich
Tel: (06723) 8090
Large, but attractive and comfortable hotel situated close to the bank of the Rhine. Conveniently central for those staying longer.

RESTAURANTS

Restaurant Graues Haus
Graugasse 10
D 65375 Winkel
Tel: (06723) 2619
Since arriving at the Graues Haus 15 years ago, talented Egbert Ebgelhardt's innovative modern cuisine has gone from strength to strength. The precisely judged flavours and textures and the amazing sauces clearly make this the region's top restaurant. The dishes need, and deserve, time to be fully appreciated. The wine list offers all that is good in the Rheingau; ask for the rarities list, which goes back to 1921.

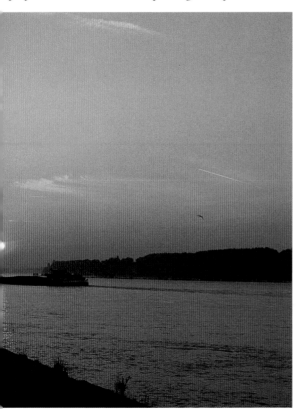

Above *The small chapel between the Schonhell and Würzgarten vineyards, north of Hallgarten, close to Hattenheim. There are few more fittingly tranquil settings than that made by the vines and gently rolling landscape here.*

HATTENHEIM

Hattenheim is one of the most beautiful and famous winegrowing villages of the Rheingau. Driving from the centre of Oestrich, and before entering the village, you pass the 18th-century Schloss Reichartshausen on the right, with its folly ruin and two pagodas decorating the garden. Its vineyards are a monopoly run by the Balthasar Ress estate. Directly next to Schloss Reichartshausen stands the walled Pfaffenberg site, a monopoly of Schloss Schönborn. Below the railway line that bisects the village lies old Hattenheim, with the ruined, medieval Hattenheimer Burg, home to the Langwerth von Simmern family until 1711, and the imposing estate house of Graf Schönborn (the Schloss Schönborn estate). At the centre of old Hattenheim stands a

cluster of old houses, including the Hotel/Restaurant zum Krug, whose decorated half-timbered frontage is the finest surviving example of the house-painting style that was once common throughout the region.

Hattenheim's name is inseparable from those of its two greatest vineyards, the Nussbrunnen and Wisselbrunnen, which lie above the railway line on the town's eastern side. As their names indicate, both these vineyards are planted around springs (*Brunnen*). The underground sources of water mean that, as in the world-famous Marcobrunn site a few hundred metres away, even in the hottest summers the local soils do not dry out. This, together with the deep marl upon which the vines stand, is a recipe for powerful, complex wines with the structure for long ageing.

HATTENHEIM

RECOMMENDED PRODUCERS

Weingut Hans Lang
Rheinallee 6, D 65347 Hattenheim
Tel: (06723) 2475
Medium-sized estate with consistent, good-quality wines that never lack substance or balance. Appointment recommended; essential weekends.

Domänenweingut Schloss Schönborn
Hauptstrasse 53, D 65347 Hattenheim
Tel: (06723) 2007
One of the region's most famous names. Currently struggling to regain lost form after problems in the 1990s. Big, powerful wines. By appointment only; closed weekends.

Weingut Hans Barth
Bergweg 20, D 65347 Hattenheim
Tel: (06723) 2514
Dynamic estate best-known for its Ultra Sekt, one of Germany's finest sparkling wines. The still Rieslings are all very clean, but of mixed quality. Appointment recommended; closed Sunday.

Weingut Balthasar Ress
Rheinallee 7, D 65347 Hattenheim
Tel: (06723) 3011
Large estate with vineyards stretching from Rüdesheim to Hochheim. Its wines are made for drinking young.

HOTELS

Hotel Kronenschlösschen
Rheinallee, D 65347 Hattenheim
Tel: (06723) 640
This excellent hotel offers architectural splendour and luxury. The cooking is modern and of good quality. The bistro-restaurant is one of the best of its kind in the region.

Hotel zum Krug
Hauptstrasse 34, D 65347 Hattenheim
Tel: (06723) 99680
Although partly in a half-timbered house dating from 1720, the rooms are comfortable and rustic without being old-fashioned. The restaurant offers traditional regional cooking. The list of Rheingau wines is impressive, the prices modest.

RESTAURANTS

Hotel Kronenschlösschen
See hotels.

Adler Wirtschaft
Hauptstrasse 31, D 65347 Hattenheim
Tel: (06723) 7982
Franz Keller's unique pub offers country cooking of the highest standard and a fine selection of German, French and Italian wines in a stylish modern interior. Make reservations or risk a lengthy wait.

KLOSTER EBERBACH

RECOMMENDED PRODUCERS

Weingut Prinz
Im Flachsgarten 5
D 65375 Hallgarten
Tel: (06723) 7924
The wines from Fred Prinz's mini-estate prove that little-known Hallgarten can challenge the Rheingau's most famous wine villages. Both the dry and naturally sweet Rieslings are of very good quality. Strictly by appointment; closed Sunday.

Weingut Adam Nass-Englemann
Hallgartener Platz 2
D 65375 Hallgarten
Tel: (06723) 3366
A small estate with a modest range of racy, dry wines; older vintages are also available. By appointment only; closed Sunday.

Weingut Jakob Riedel
Taunusstrasse 1
D 65375 Hallgarten
Tel: (06723) 3511
Riedel produces extreme wines of a hit-and-miss quality. The best are bone-dry Rieslings with an intense minerally character. Strictly by appointment.

KLOSTER EBERBACH

The former Cistercian abbey of Kloster Eberbach stands three kilometres above Hattenheim and is one of the great cultural monuments of the Rheingau. It was founded by the mystic Bernhard von Clairvaux in 1136, and from the beginning, wine production played an important role in the monastery's functions. In 1232, monks finished laying out the famous Steinberg vineyard between the abbey and Hattenheim; by the end of the 13th century, they had become the world's largest wine producers. In 1766, they completed the construction of the three-kilometre long wall which surrounds the Steinberg, making it the German equivalent of Burgundy's Clos Vougeot. In poor vintages, the wines here can be steely and sharp, while those produced in hot years can possess a sensational elegance and aromatic subtlety. Today, Kloster Eberbach is the base of the Rheingau's *Staatsweingüter*, or state domaine, which solely owns the Steinberg vineyard. Unfortunately at present, these wines rarely live up to the legend.

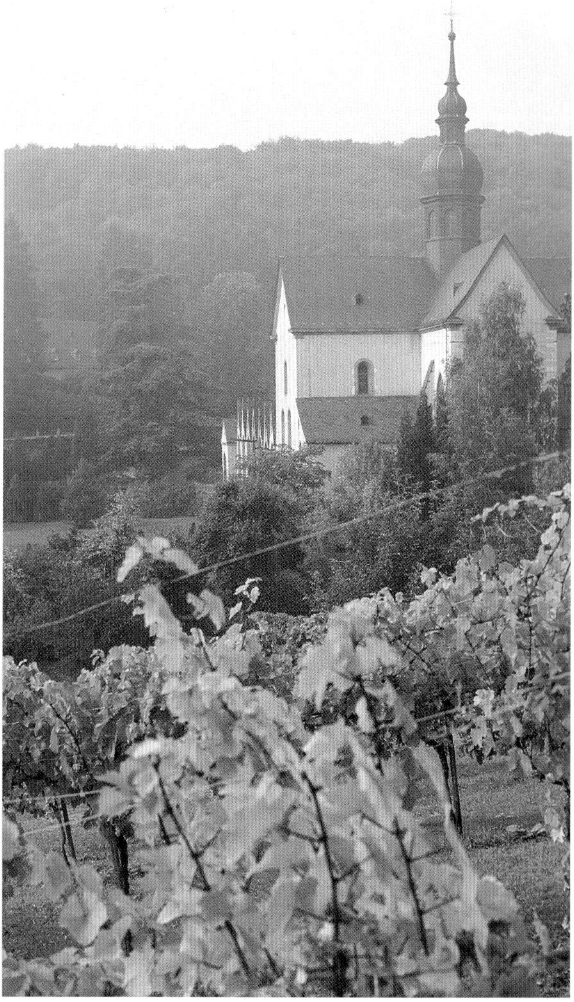

Right *Kloster Eberbach in Hattenheim. A 12th century monastery, now the home home of the German Wine Academy and the state domaine.*
Far right *Autumn arriving in the famous Steinberg vineyard, which stretches between Kloster Eberbach and Hattenheim.*

Because of the sheer size of the monastery – it was in effect a self-sufficient community, complete with its own hospital – you need plenty of time to explore fully Kloster Eberbach's extensive complex of stone halls and galleries. The most imposing of these is the 72-metre long *Mönchsdormitorium*, or monks' dormitory, which at one time would have housed close to 300 monks. Beneath it lies the Kabinett-Keller, where legendary wines, such as the 1811 Steinberger, were matured.

The monumental Romanesque *Klosterkirche*, or monastery chuch, is the oldest part of the abbey, having been consecrated by the archbishop of Mainz on May 23, 1186. The collection of over 80 medieval *Grabplatten* (tombstones) of bishops, abbots and knights helps one grasp the span of time in which these walls have stood. The remarkable acoustics of the church, where sounds echo for as long as eight seconds, can be most fully appreciated during the series of classical concerts that are staged here each summer.

Below *Directions are given in Hattenheim, so that visitors can find all the wine cellars.*

Left *Views over the Grafenberg vines and Burg Scharfenstein to the historical village of Kiedrich. Grass growing between the vine rows is competition: it makes the vine roots search deeper for better and more constant water supply.*

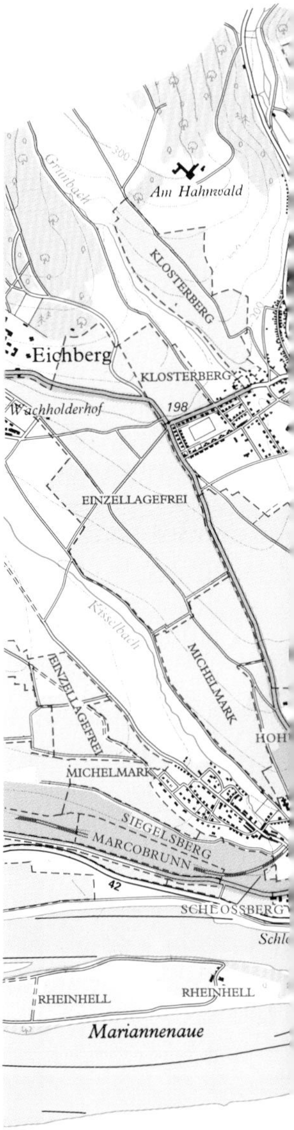

KIEDRICH

Gothic and Renaissance styles most strongly distinguish the nearby wine village of Kiedrich. The village's location is idyllic: the elegant spire of the Saint Valentinkirche rises against the backdrop of the famous Gräfenberg vineyard, which is crowned by the ruined Burg Scharfenstein. The church and the *Michaelskapelle* (Saint Michael's Chapel) which stand nearby are among the graceful examples of Germany's High Gothic style. The organ in Saint Valentinkirche is the oldest in Germany, dating from the late-15th century (although some of its pipes go back to 1312). The church also contains a wealth of carvings and statues from both the Gothic and Renaissance periods.

The major Renaissance monument in the village is the stone-built *Rathaus* (Town Hall), which was completed in 1586. A few yards away in Suttonstrasse is a row of imposing houses, the most magnificent of which is the Baroque Schwalbacher Hof, designed by Anselm Freiherr von Ritter zu Groenesteyn in 1730; it is occupied by the von Ritter family to this day. The Baroque Bassenheimer Hof and Eberbacher Hof are also worth a visit.

Vinously, Kiedrich is dominated by the famous Robert Weil estate. Its architecture is Neo-Gothic, the Weil estate house having been constructed between 1878 and 1906. The complex of buildings was considerably extended with the introduction of new cellars in the early 1990s, which have been beautifully integrated into the whole. However, not only does director Wilhelm Weil have the most modern winemaking cellars in the region, the excellent wines his estate produces define contemporary Rheingau Riesling. Today, the estate's Auslese, BA and TBA wines are among the most sought-after in Germany – just as they were a century ago. The 1893 Auslese was bought by the royal houses of Germany, Austria and England for astronomical prices, and the 1992 TBA Gold Cap recently set a world record for the most expensive young wine of any kind.

KIEDRICH

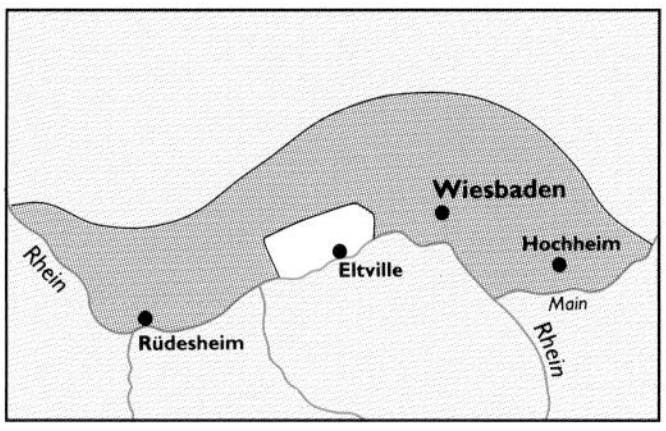

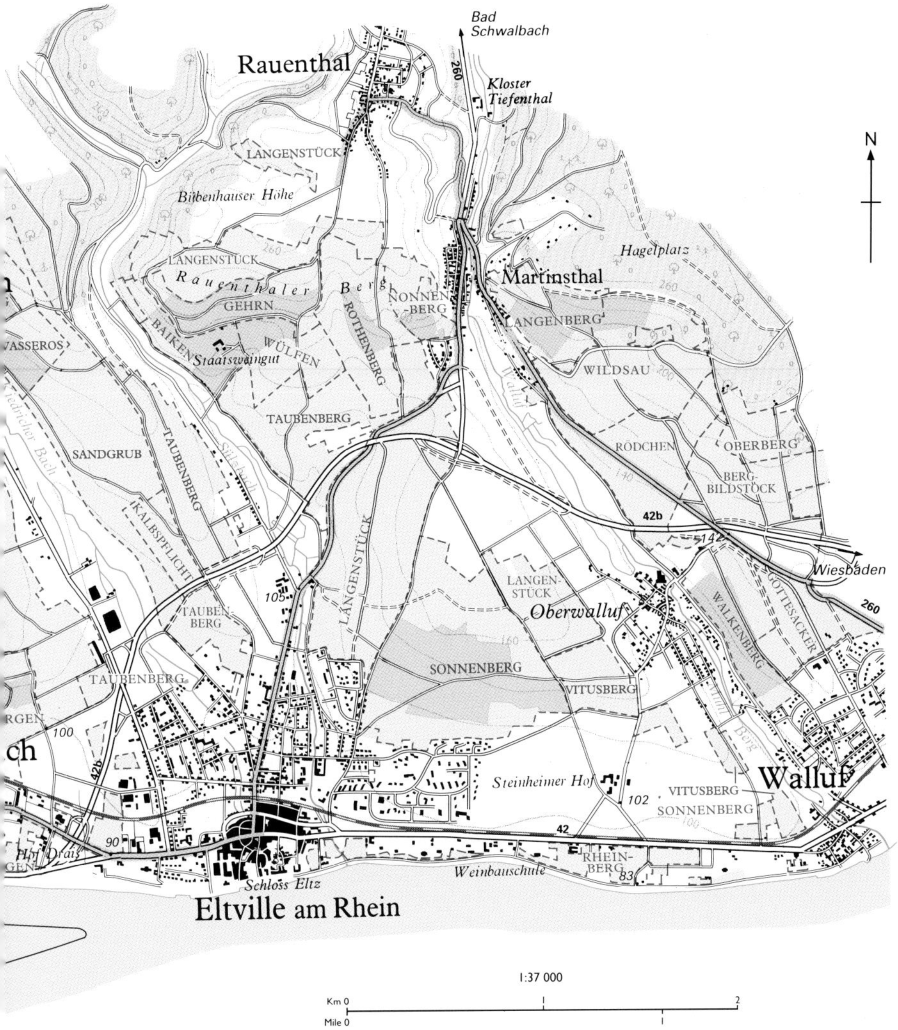

1:37 000

Km 0 1 2
Mile 0 1

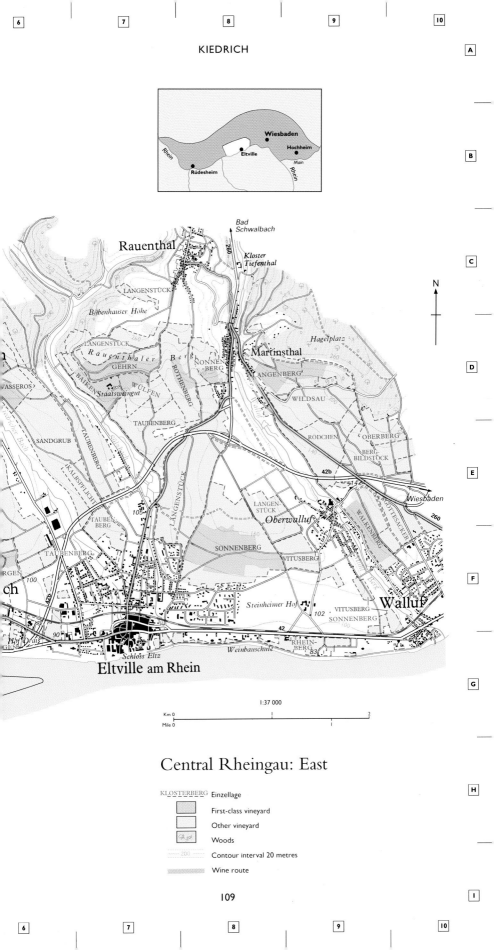

Central Rheingau: East

KLOSTERBERG Einzellage

First-class vineyard

Other vineyard

Woods

200 Contour interval 20 metres

Wine route

These wines all came from the Gräfenberg vineyard of Kiedrich. Besides being one of the Rheingau's most beautiful vineyards, the Gräfenberg is also one of its greatest. Its slate soil gives Rieslings their richness and body – even opulence. The wines always remain perfectly poised and precisely balanced, and frequently possess intense mineral or herbal notes. Even when the vintage is one inclined to leanness and tartness, they never have an aggressive acidity.

From Kiedrich, follow the signs to Erbach, just three kilometres away.

ERBACH

Erbach's reputation comes almost entirely from just one of its vineyards: the world-famous Marcobrunn. In 1726, it became the first vineyard name to appear on the label of a bottled German wine. To reach the Marcobrunn, on arriving in Erbach from Kiedrich turn right in the centre of town. Pass the late-Gothic church of Saint Markus on the right and the Schloss Reinhartshausen wine estate and luxury hotel on the left. The first block of vines on your right are the Schlossberg, a monopoly run by Schloss Reinhartshausen. The great sweep of the Marcobrunn begins after the little lane running to the right under the railway line. In its centre stands the spring which gives the vineyard its name. The Neo-Classical monument surrounding the spring was erected in 1810 by the people of Erbach, shortly after American president and vinophile Thomas Jefferson had sung the praises of the Marcobrunn wines. A legend, it seems, was already in the making.

Like several of the Rheingau's other famous vineyards, however, the Marcobrunn has become a double-edged sword for the region's vintners in recent years. Every good wine from this famous site adds an aura of success to other wines

Right *Erbach is famed for just one of its vineyards, but the striking church of St-Markus (among other features) shows that there is more to it.* Top right *Eltville is aristocratic in every way: not least in its houses.*

KIEDRICH

RECOMMENDED PRODUCERS

Weingut Robert Weil
Mühlberg 5, D 65399 Kiedrich
Tel: (06123) 2308
Enormous investments from Japanese owner Suntory, and director Wilhelm Weil's tireless pursuit of quality have put Robert Weil at the forefront of the Rheingau. High standards are maintained with the sleek, dry Rieslings and the naturally sweet wines. Appointment recommended; essential at weekends.

HOTELS

Nassauer Hof
Bingerpfortenstrasse 17
D 65399 Kiedrich
Tel: (06123) 2476
A pleasant, comfortable hotel at the edge of Kiedrich with a pleasant, unpretentious restaurant.

RESTAURANTS

Gutsschänke Schloss Groenesteyn
Oberstrasse 36, D 65399 Kiedrich
Tel: (06123) 1533
Popular wine bar of this estate. The rustic food is better than the wines.

ERBACH

RECOMMENDED PRODUCERS

Weingut Schloss Reinhartshausen
D 65346 Erbach
Tel: (06123) 676333
Classical, dry Rheingau Rieslings. The *Halbtrocken* (half-dry) wines are often excellent; Riesling Spätlesen and Auslesen often first-class. The wine shop is open every day except Sunday. Tours by appointment only.

Weingut Freiherr zu Knyphausen
Klosterhof Drais, D 65346 Erbach
Tel: (06123) 62177
Good-quality, traditional-style Rheingau Rieslings; very good Charta wines; excellent Auslesen. Appointment recommended; closed Sunday.

Weingut Jakob Jung
Eberbacherstr 22, D 65346 Erbach
Tel: (06123) 62359
Ludwig Jung makes racy, dry Rieslings of improving quality. Open for tastings from 3.30pm; appointment recommended; closed Sunday.

in surrounding areas. Every poor wine sold is a boomerang which lands in the face of its producer, indirectly damaging the name of his or her town and region into the bargain. In recent years, there have been many substandard Marcobrunners, and very few that have been worthy of the name (look for Schloss Reinhartshausen and Freiherr zu Knyphausen's wines).

The deep marl soil of the vineyard yields successful Marcobrunn wines, big and powerful with a very firm structure. In their youth these wines are often unforthcoming, but with several years of ageing they acquire an intense, many-faceted bouquet and flavour in which fruit, mineral and spice notes mingle in harmony. The neighbouring Siegelsberg and Schlossberg vineyards yield similar, if slightly lighter, more charming wines. At their best, they can equal anything from the Marcobrunn. The wines from Erbach's other vineyards are rather less dramatic, but combine raciness with subtle peachy fruit.

ELTVILLE

Drive back through Erbach and pass the 19th-century Neo-Gothic Protestant church on the left and the early 18th-century Klosterhof Drais, home of the Freiherr zu Knyphausen estate, on the right as you leave town. Eltville is separated from Erbach only by the Autobahn bypass, which has saved Eltville's old, narrow streets from the traffic that used to choke them. The oldest part of town is that between the main road and the river bank. Here lies the town's Burg, the castle that was the Archbishop of Mainz's residence from 1330 to 1480. It tempted many aristocratic families to build in Elville, most notably those of Graf Eltz and Freiherr von Simmern, whose extensive residences are beautifully preserved.

While Eltville may lack the high points of some of the other wine-growing Rheingau communities, its Sonnenberg vineyards yield attractive, fruity wines. Whether produced in the dry or naturally sweet versions, they make an excellent introduction to the regional style.

Winzergenossenschaft Erbach
Ringstrasse 28, D 65346 Erbach
Tel: (06123) 62414
The Rheingau's best cooperative winery makes light, fruity wines at modest prices. Also well-made BA, TBA. Appointment recommended.

HOTELS

Hotel Schloss Reinhartshausen
Hauptstrasse 43, D 65337 Erbach
Tel: (06123) 6760
Luxury hotel for those seeking comfort in the grand style. Cavernous suites, acres of marble, an astonishing collection of paintings and prices to match. The sophisticated, modern cooking of Joachim Wissler in the Marcobrunn restaurant is also impressive. In the Schlosskeller restaurant, the food is simpler but also good and prices more moderate.

RESTAURANTS

Marcobrunn/Schlosskeller
See Hotel Schloss Reinhartshausen.

Pan zu Erbach
Eberbacherstrasse 44
D 65346 Erbach
Tel: (06123) 63538
Angelika Heckl's restaurant may be difficult to find, but the search is worth it for modern Italianate cooking.

ELTVILLE

RECOMMENDED PRODUCERS

Weingut Okonomierat J Fischer Erben
Weinhole 14, D 65347 Eltville
Tel: (06123) 2858
Deliberately old-fashioned wines with plenty of character and very good ageing potential. Appointment only.

Weingut Freiherr Langwerth von Simmern
Kirchgasse/Langwerther Hof
D 65343 Eltville
Tel: (06123) 3007
Legendary estate having a tough job regaining form after poor vintages in the early '90s. Concentration and elegance were hallmarks. Appointment recommended; closed weekends.

Verwaltung der Staatsweingüter Kloster Eberbach
Schwalbacherstrasse 56–62
D 65343 Eltville
Tel: (06123) 61055
The region's largest estate, owning most of the best vineyards on the Rauenthaler Berg and all of the Steinberg, but often disappointing wine quality. Dessert wines are best, but expensive. Tasting room open Monday to Friday; Saturday mornings.

MARTINSTHAL

RECOMMENDED PRODUCERS

Weingut Diefenhardt
Hauptstrasse 11
D 65344 Martinsthal
Tel: (06123) 71490
A small estate making good Rieslings from the vineyards of Martinsthal and Rauenthal. By appointment only.

Weingut Peter Kessler
Heimatstrasse 18
D 65344 Martinsthal
Tel: (06123) 72430
Another small estate with erratic quality, but some good dry wines. By appointment only.

WALLUF

RECOMMENDED PRODUCERS

Weingut J B Becker
Rheinstrasse 6
D 65396 Walluf
Tel: (06123) 72523
Brother and sister Hans-Josef and Maria Becker concentrate on serious dry Rieslings; also good Auslesen and higher Prädikat wines, and some fine Spätburgunder reds. Appointment recommended; essential weekends. Wine garden is open May to October from 5pm; at weekends from 3pm.

RAUENTHAL AND MARTINSTHAL

Take the Schwalbacherstrasse from the centre of Eltville to Rauenthal, and you'll pass the winery of the Rheingau Staatsweingüter on the left (Schwalbacherstrasse 58–64) before leaving town. Rauenthal is worth a visit, both to see its famous vineyards and to enjoy the magnificent view from the peak of the Rauenthaler Berg, more than 150 metres above the river. Just past the road under the Eltville bypass you will see the Rauenthaler Berg in its entirety. Rauenthal's are some of the finest vineyards on the Rhine, and during the late-19th and early-20th centuries, their names became synonymous with all that is great in Rheingau wine. This was due largely to the work of the erstwhile Royal Prussian Domaine which, since 1945, has become known as the Staatsweingüter Kloster Eberbach.

As the road turns towards Martinsthal, you'll be able to see that the Staatsweingut buildings are surrounded by substantial vineyard holdings, including most of the Baiken and Gehrn sites. The generally poor standard of the wines here makes good Rauenthal Rieslings quite hard to find, another tragic example of the Rheingau's present winemaking malaise. Currently, the only Rauenthal Rieslings that possess the combination of elegance, depth and minerally spice which once made the wines from these vineyards so famous, come only from the Georg Breuer estate of Rüdesheim and from August Eser of Oestrich.

The names of Martinsthal's vineyards are virtually unknown, although the Langenberg can produce wines similar to those of Rauenthal's best, and the amusingly named *Wildsau* (wild sow) also yields good wines. The village of Martinsthal nestles between the Langenberg vineyard on the right and the Rauenthaler Nonnenberg vineyard on the left, a monopoly of Georg Breuer, together with the mid-19th-century, twin-towered Villa Nonnenberg. As you leave Martinsthal on the B260 (direction Bad Schwalbach), look for the small road that winds its way up to Rauenthal. To reach Bad Schwalbach, continue on from here.

Rauenthal has a certain austerity, never having been one of the region's wealthiest or most immediately appealing villages, and it cannot boast any important wine producers. Walk out from the viewing point on the Bubenhäuser Höhe. From here you can see over the Rheingau as far as Oestrich-Winkel, and over the river to Rheinhessen and Mainz on the opposite bank.

Turn back along the B260 to the junction with the B42, turning right here back in the direction of Rüdesheim to reach the centre of Walluf. And what better way to end a long day's touring than a glass or two of wine in the wine garden of Walluf's J B Becker estate, on the bank of the Rhine? Walluf has a strong tradition of Spätburgunder red-wine production, and its Walkenberg site delivers elegant, well-structured Rieslings and Spätburgunders. From here it is only a short drive to Wiesbaden or Mainz.

HOTELS

Hotel Ruppert
Hauptstrasse 61
D 65396 Walluf
Tel: (06123) 71089
A conveniently situated hotel with simple but pleasant rooms.

RESTAURANTS

Restaurant Schwann
Rheinstrasse 4
D 65396 Walluf
Tel: (06123) 72410
Serves traditional regional cooking of a good standard – and not a single piece of designer furniture to be seen in the Wilhelmine interior. A good selection of Rheingau wines.

Below left *Autumnal vineyards surrounding the state wine cellars in Rauenthal: these are 'Baiken' vines as seen from the 'Gehrn' Einzellage.*
Below *Hope for a clearer day than this when you climb to the Rauenthaler Berg, over 150 metres above the river, as there are some fabulous views to be had.*

WIESBADEN

HOTELS

Nassauer Hof
Kaiser-Friedrich-Platz 3–4
D 65183 Wiesbaden
Tel: (0611) 1330
Excellent luxury hotel for money-no-object travellers. Boasts everything you would expect from a five-star hotel, plus has direct access to Wiesbaden's spa.

Hotel Schwarzer Bock (Radisson SAS)
Kranzplatz 12
D 65183 Wiesbaden
Tel: (0611) 1550
Founded in 1486, this is the oldest hotel in Germany, excellent in a traditional style, with a marvellous bar and good restaurant (also rather traditional) called Capricorne, whose wine list offers a large selection of Rheingau and French wines.

Hotel de France
Taunusstrasse 49
D 65183 Wiesbaden
Tel: (0611) 520061
Comfortable, moderately priced hotel in central Wiesbaden.

RESTAURANTS

Die Ente vom Lehl/ Bistro Ente vom Lehl
Kaiser-Friedrich-Platz 3–4
D 65183 Wiesbaden
Tel: (0611) 133666
'The Duck from Lehl' is a grand restaurant with excellent modern cooking and a sensational list of German and French wines (consult Sommelier Kai Schattner). For those who don't want to burden the credit card too heavily, the downstairs bistro offers a less-spectacular version of Herbert Langendorf's cuisine. Here, too, the full wine list is available.

Brasserie Bruno
Taunusstrasse 49
D 65183 Wiesbaden
Tel: (0611) 51251
Extremely popular bistro offering a mix of German, French and Italian cooking.

Restaurant Capricorne
See Hotel Schwarzer Bock.

WIESBADEN

The most eastern vineyards of the Rheingau – those of Hochheim – are separated from the main body of the region by the town of Wiesbaden. Even the casual visitor will quickly spot that there is plenty of old money here. Its innumerable grand villas, imposing spa house, state theatre and casino all speak volumes about its stylishness and elegance. If money poses no problem, Wiesbaden makes an ideal base for touring the Rheingau and surrounding regions. But even for those on a more limited budget, the town is worth a stop for its star restaurant, Die Ente vom Lehl, the Neroberg hill upon which the town's single vineyard stands, and the Wiesbaden *Weinwoche*, or 'wine week'. In the third week of August, the pedestrian zone in the town centre is given over to a wine-and-food festival without comparison in Germany. Only Rheingau wine is served (many of the best estates have stands), and the food on offer ranges from the traditional to modern.

HOCHHEIM

The wine town of Hochheim is the opposite of Wiesbaden: it is down-to-earth and quite unpretentious. Though the A671 Autobahn passes over the vineyards on a flyover, and modern developments on the outskirts of Hochheim have done nothing to make the town more attractive, the Altstadt remains unspoilt, and boasts many fine 17th- and 18th-century houses.

Hochheim's vineyards lie on the right bank of the River Main just before it flows into the Rhine, and they benefit from the warmth of both rivers. The best of them – the Domdechaney, Kirchenstück and Hölle – have much heavier soils than the rest of the region, which produces powerful wines with a firm core. For best results, these wines need years of age, and the finest can live for decades. No wonder, then, that they were among the most highly sought-after Rheingau wines a century ago. It also comes as no surprise that the name for all Rhine wines in the English language – 'Hock' – derives from Hochheim's wares.

The town's special relationship with England was also cemented by the Königin Victoria Berg vineyard (effectively

Right *The Domdechaney vineyard at Hochheim: wines from these vines are firm, full and powerful – this is due to their nearness to the River Main, giving relatively heavy soils and a warm climate of reflected sun.*

part of the Hölle site). After Queen Victoria visited Hochheim in the summer of 1850, the owner of the vines, G M Pabstmann, requested that the vineyard where the Queen sampled the first ripe grapes of the year be named after her. When permission was granted, Pabstmann erected an extraordinary mock-Tudor monument in Queen Victoria's honour (it has recently been restored), and then created an Neo-Gothic label depicting it. Today, the monument is owned by Oestrich's Hupfeld estate.

The two estates that currently contend for the title of Hochheim's leading producer are the long-established member of the Rheingau elite, Domdechant Werner'sches Weingut, and a new arrival, Weingut Franz Künstler. At least for dry Rieslings, there can be no question that the crown goes to Künstler, who makes the grandest dry wines in the region.

Sadly, the most important vineyard owners in Hochheim (Staatsweingüter and Schloss Schönborn) are not actually based here, but are elsewhere in the Rheingau, in Kloster Eberbach/Eltville and Hattenheim. For them, Hochheim comes a long way down the list of priorities – which is a shame, considering the area's potential. They will have to do much better if Hochheim's wines are ever to regain the good reputation they enjoyed a century ago.

HOCHHEIM

RECOMMENDED PRODUCERS

Weingut Franz Künstler
Freiherr-von-Stein-Ring 3
D 65239 Hochheim
Tel: (06146) 82570
Gunter Künstler makes some of the most concentrated and sophisticated dry Rieslings in all of Germany in the cellars of this unpretentious, suburban house. Strictly by appointment; no tastings on weekday mornings.

Domdechant Werner'sches Weingut
Rathausstrasse 30, D 65239 Hochheim
Tel: (06146) 2008
Well-known estate making elegant, medium-bodied Rieslings in both dry and naturally sweet styles. Particularly good value at the Spätlese level. By appointment only; closed Sundays.

Weingut Heinrich Baison
Delkenheimerstrasse 18
D 65239 Hochheim
Tel: (06146) 9232
Small estate making substantial dry wines with plenty of character. By appointment only.

Weingut Joachim Flick
D 65439 Flörsheim (nr Hochheim)
Tel: (06145) 6468
Small estate making clean, modern style wines. Estate's wine bar is open March to July and September to November from 4pm (except Monday and Tuesday). Otherwise appointment recommended; closed Sundays.

RESTAURANTS

Restaurant Nassauer Hof
Delkenheimer Strasse 1
D 6203 Hochheim
Tel: (06146) 5326
The best address in Hochheim. Traditional French and German cooking of a good standard. Some good wines, too.

Above *Hochheim's Altstadt – retaining its peacefulness and charm despite the surrounding busyness of the rest of the town.*
Left *The monument at the Königin Victoriaberg vineyard, celebrating the popularity of its wines in the UK and Queen Victoria's visit.*

Rheinhessen

The name Rheinhessen does not spark off associations in the minds of wine lovers as does, say, the mention of the Mosel or the Rheingau. Yet this region possesses some of the finest vineyards on the Rhine, and produces some of the greatest wines in Germany. Indeed, some of its dry and dessert Rieslings put virtually everything produced in the Rheingau in the shade.

Rheinhessen's problem is its size and the diversity of its wines. Most of the region consists of a wide expanse of hill country from Mainz west to the Nahe, and from the left bank of the Rhine facing the Rheingau south to Worms. Apart from where Autobahns snake across its undulating contours in an ungainly fashion, this is an attractive, if undramatic, landscape. Two small 'islands' stand out of this sea of vines and fields: the steep vineyards of Bingen, at the region's northwestern extremity, and the sweeping slopes close to Nierstein, just south of Mainz. As in so many parts of Germany, the wines of Rheinhessen closely reflect their landscape, and it is Bingen and the Nierstein area which produce the most dramatic wines in the region.

Nierstein has done more to make Rheinhessen famous than any other winegrowing community in the region, and this has led to the merciless exploitation of its name. The first Beerenauslese and Trockenbeerenauslese wines were produced here in 1893 by the Franz Karl Schmitt estate. In the 1960s, Nierstein's top growers continued to enjoy a high reputation for their Rieslings. But the town's growers started to rest on their laurels, using sweetness as a substitute for wine quality; then the 1971 wine law delivered an almost fatal blow by creating the Grosslage Niersteiner Gutes Domtal.

Wines from more than a dozen villages close to Nierstein (with vineyards greatly inferior to its own) are allowed to sell their wines under this name. They line

Left *The slopes of the Brudersberg vineyard with their treasured Riesling vines. The steepness and red slate soil give the wines their distinctive minerally nature, prized by the winemakers of nearby Nackenheim* (above).

supermarket shelves in the UK, Holland and in many other markets where there is considerable demand for cheap, sweet wines with little or no character. The effect on Nierstein's and Rheinhessen's reputation for quality has been disastrous.

Coupled with this fact, the quality renaissance that has affected all of Germany's winegrowing regions in recent years did not actually reach Rheinhessen until the latter half of the 1980s. In places, the results have already been dramatic, but so far the number of new star producers is rather small – too small to kick-start a quality movement throughout the region as a whole. One often feels that most of Rheinhessen's inhabitants are unaware of the riches that their region has to offer. The towns of Mainz and Worms have a number of obvious historic monuments, but who talks about the wealth of history to be found in the towns and villages surrounding them? In addition, Rheinhessen's fertile soils and warm climate mean that a wide range of fruits and vegetables flourish here. The region may not be able to boast a single Michelin restaurant star, but there are a large number of inns and country restaurants that turn Rheinhessen's products into tasty dishes. Most of them only await discovery, and it is a wise wine tourist who actually takes time to do so.

Below *Vineyards of the 'red slope' or Roter Hang – Brudersberg and Hipping – renowned (as many in the area are) for their fine Riesling wines.*

6
7
8
9
10
A
B
C
D
E
F
G
H
I
N
Wiesbaden
Budenheim
Mombach
Heidenfahrt
A643
Gonsenheim
MAINZ
Heidesheim
Finthen
A60
Wackernheim
Bretzenheim
Weisenau
Rüsselsheim
Drais
E42
Ingelheim
Ingelheim Sud
Lerchenberg
Laubenheim
Marienborn
Hechtsheim
Gross-Winternheim
Ober-Olm
Klein-Winternheim
Rhein
Selz
Essenheim
Bodenheim
232
Elsheim
Ebersheim
Nackenheim
Stadecken
Gau-Bischofsheim
Nieder-Olm
Harxheim
Engelstadt
Pfadberg 203
A63
Lörzweiler
Jugenheim
Zornheim
Mommenheim
Sörgenloch
Saulheim
Nierstein
Schwabsburg
Vendersheim
Udenheim
Selzen
Hahnheim
Oppenheim
Schornsheim
Köngernheim
Sulzheim
420
Dexheim
Dienheim
Wörrstadt
Undenheim
Friesenheim
Gabsheim
Dalheim
Rommersheim
Schimsheim
271
Weinolsheim
Spiesheim
Uelversheim
Ludwigshöhe
Ensheim
Bechtolsheim
Biebelnheim
Petersberg 245
Eimsheim
Guntersblum
Gau-Odernheim
Dolgesheim
Bornheim
Bermersheim
Gimbsheim
Albig
Gau-Köngernheim
Hillesheim
Wintersheim
Dorn-Dürkheim
Schafhausen
Framersheim
Frettenheim
Alsheim
Dittelsheim
Eich
Dautenheim
Alzey
Gau-Heppenheim
Hessloch
Mettenheim
Bechtheim
Hamm
Hochborn
Monzernheim
Kettenheim
Wahlheim
Esselborn
Ibersheim
Hangen-Weisheim
Osthofen
Dintesheim
Eppelsheim
Freimersheim
Westhofen
Rhein-dürkheim
Flomborn
Gundersheim
Ilbesheim
Ober-Flörsheim
Bermersheim
Abenheim
Gundheim
296
Mörstadt
A61
E31
Flörsheim-Dalsheim
Niederflörsheim
Neuhausen
Herrnsheim
Zell
Mölsheim
Leiselheim
Wachenheim
Kriegsheim
Hochheim
Pfeddersheim
47
Pfrimm
Monsheim
Pfiffligheim
WORMS
Hohen-Sülzen
Kindenheim
Bockenheim
Offstein
Heppenheim
Wiesoppenheim
Weinsheim
Neuoffstein
Obrigheim
Ludwigshafen
Colgenstein
Heidesheim
Albsheim

MAINZ

HOTELS

Hilton International
Rheinstrasse 68, D 55116 Mainz
Tel: (06131) 2450
Those looking for luxury couldn't do better in Rheinhessen than to book into this comfortable, modern hotel.

RESTAURANTS

Battenheimer Hof
Rheinstrasse 2, D 55294 Bodenheim
Tel: (06135) 7090
Pleasant country hotel on a wine estate in Bodenheim, just south of Mainz. Excellent value for money.

PLACES OF INTEREST

Mainz has several important cultural monuments. The Romanesque cathedral still dominates the town, the post-1945 reconstruction around it is not a worthy frame. The Gutenberg Museum (Liebfrauenplatz) contains the first printed Bible. Also in the town centre, the Gothic church of St-Stephan (Stephansplatz) wiith marvellous stained glass windows by Marc Chagall, and the Baroque Prince Bishop's Schloss houses the Römisch-Germanisches Museum with a fine collection of artefacts from the Roman period to the Middle Ages.

NACKENHEIM

RECOMMENDED PRODUCERS

Weingut Gunderloch
Carl-Gunderloch-Platz 1
D 55299 Nackenheim
Tel: (06135) 2341
The intensely fruity, concentrated Rieslings made here are among the greatest Rhine wines made today. Even the standard dry Rieslings and Jean-Baptiste Kabinetts marry racy elegance with seductive fruit; the Spätlesen and higher Prädikat wines are masterpieces of richness, depth and balance. Strictly by appointment.

RESTAURANTS

Restaurant Gunderloch
Carl-Gunderloch-Platz 1
D 55299 Nackenheim
Tel: (06135) 2341
Country cooking of exceptional quality; wines from the Gunderloch estate at extremely attractive prices.

Weingut Nack
Pfarrstr 13, D 55296 Gau-Bischofsheim
Tel: (06135) 3043
Restaurant with high ambitions housed in a tastefully decorated ex-barrel cellar.

NACKENHEIM

Take the B9 south from Mainz to reach Rheinhessen's small collection of great vineyards. These begin at Nackenheim, which was made famous by the wine estate of Carl Gunderloch at the beginning of the 20th century. His 1911 Riesling Trockenbeerenauslese from the Nackenheimer Rothenberg vineyard became the most expensive wine in the region's history when it was auctioned in 1913 for 15 Goldmarks per bottle.

In 1925, Carl Zuckmayer's play, *The Merry Vineyard,* immortalized Carl Gunderloch under the name Jean-Baptiste, causing a rift between Zuckmayer and the Gunderlochs which lasted decades. Now the estate honours Zuckmayer with its excellent Jean-Baptiste Riesling Kabinett. Since the beginning of the 1990s, the Gunderloch estate has been at peak performance, making the finest Riesling wines in the region. Appropriately, Riesling TBA from the Rothenberg is the most expensive wine in Rheinhessen. Today, the centre of Nackenheim is still pretty much as Zuckmayer must have known it, particularly the Carl Zuckmayer Platz with its half-timbered Rathaus and other buildings.

Immediately to the south of Nackenheim, the *Roter Hang*, or 'red slope' begins. This is the site of the steepest vineyards in Rheinhessen, which rise more than a hundred metres almost directly from the left bank of the Rhine. The soil is a type of red slate that quickly weathers to a mineral-rich, red earth. It gives the Riesling wines that grow here a silkiness and aromatic richness that is as seductive as it is refined. Low yields result in extremely concentrated wines which are impressive in the dry as well as the naturally sweet styles. The local Riesling dessert wines are truly phenomenal.

Each of the vineyard sites that make up the Roter Hang yields distinctive Rieslings. Following the slope from its north extremity to its southwestern tip: the Rothenberg wines are slow-developing with a combination of lavish fruit and a structure that ages for decades; those from the Pettental are more charming and elegant, developing an intense minerally character with age; the Brudersberg (a Heyl zu Herrnsheim monopoly) yields the most elegant and refined wines; those from the Hipping are lush and exotic. Oelberg wines are powerful and deep, needing time to open up and show their best, and the Orbel yields tightly wound wines with a raciness that makes them deceptively light-footed. Today, the finest Nierstein wines are made by Saint Antony, followed by Heyl zu Herrnsheim, Heinrich Braun, Georg Albrecht Schneider, J und H A Strub and Heinrich Seebrich.

NIERSTEIN

As you approach Nierstein from the north, the town's maltings take away some of the grace from its Saint Kilianskirche, which is surrounded by the vines of the tiny Glöck vineyard. However, the Marktplatz and the narrow streets of the Altstadt are full of fine old houses dating back to the 17th century. The Mathildenhof, home to the Heyl zu Herrnsheim estate, is arguably the most imposing of them. Saint Martin's church, at the foot of the Oelberg site, offers particularly fine views of the vineyards. In the graveyard lie the Schmitts and Senfters to whom the town owes its reputation for fine Rieslings.

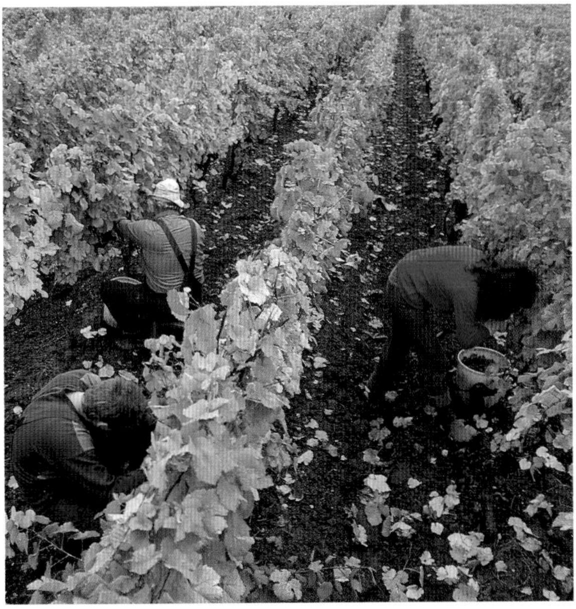

Above left *Nierstein's pretty St-Kilianskirche, surrounded by the neatly tended vines of the Glöck vineyard.*

Above *Picking Gewürztraminer grapes in Niersteiner Bildstock. Handpicking into small buckets is the gentlest possible way of collection.*

NIERSTEIN

RECOMMENDED PRODUCERS

Weingut Saint Antony
Wörrstädter Str 22, D 55283 Nierstein
Tel: (06133) 5482
Magnificent dry Rieslings: rich, even opulent, yet perfectly balanced. The only estate in Germany owned by an industrial concern to stand in the first rank. Appointment only.

Weingut Georg Albrecht Schneider
Wilhelmstrasse 6, D 55283 Nierstein
Tel: (06133) 5655
Albrecht Schneider makes lush, but beautifully crafted dry and naturally sweet Rieslings from the top sites of Nierstein. By appointment only.

Weingut Freiherr Heyl zu Herrnsheim
Langgasse 3, D 55283 Nierstein
Tel: (06133) 5120
One of Nierstein's dry wine pioneers. Rieslings, Weissburgunders and Silvaners are made in a deliberately old-fashioned style; excellent ageing potential. Appointment recommended; essential Saturdays; closed Sundays.

Weingut Heinrich Braun
Glockengasse 9, D 55283 Nierstein
Tel: (06133) 5139
Some of the best dry Rieslings in Rheinhessen. Appointment essential.

Weingut Dr Alex Senfter
Wörrstadter Str 10, D 55283 Nierstein
Tel: (06133) 5478
The best dry and naturally sweet Rieslings are full of fruit and expression. Appointment recommended.

Weingut Heinrich Seebrich
Schmiedgasse 3, D 55283 Nierstein
Tel: (06133) 58211
A very reliable source for naturally sweet Nierstein Rieslings. Appointment recommended; essential at weekends.

Weingut J und H A Strub
Rheinstrasse 42, D 55283 Nierstein
Tel: (06133) 5649
Slightly erratic, but the best naturally sweet Rieslings combine rich fruit with clarity and elegance. Appointment recommended; closed Sundays.

RESTAURANTS

Restaurant Alter Vater Rhein
Gr Fischergasse 4, D 55283 Nierstein
Tel: (06133) 5628
Rustic, kitschy restaurant in the back streets of Nierstein with hearty food.

Restaurant der halbe Mond
In der Witz 12, D 55252 Mainz-Kastel
Tel: (06134) 23913
Within easy reach of Nierstein. Inge Neu's sophisticated cooking is a little erratic, but nothing else in the Mainz area can match its best moments.

OPPENHEIM TO WORMS

PRODUCERS

Weingut Carl Koch Erben
Wormser Strasse 62
D 55276 Oppenheim
Tel: (06133) 2326
Carl Stieh-Koch makes the best wines in Oppenheim. His dry Rieslings and Weissburgunders are rich if not terribly subtle. Best are the imposing Riesling Auslese dessert wines from the Sackträger. Appointment recommended; essential weekends.

Weingut Okonomierat J Geil Erben
Kuhpfortenstrasse 11
D 67595 Bechtheim
Tel: (06242) 1546
A typical Rheinhessen estate with a dozen grape varieties, but atypically high standards. Monika and Karl Geil-Bierschenk make extremely clean, fruity dry Silvaners and Rieslings, and powerful Huxelrebe dessert wines. Appointment recommended; essential weekends.

Weingut Brüder Dr Becker
Mainzer Strasse 3
D 55278 Ludwigshöhe
Tel: (06249) 8430
Lotte Pfeffer-Müller's organic dry Rieslings and Silvaners are traditional in the best sense: racy and substantial. Her succulent, naturally sweet Scheurebe wines are the best made in the region. Appointment recommended; closed Sundays.

Weingut Kissinger
Römerstrasse 11
D 55278 Uelversheim
Tel: (06249) 7448
Ripe fruit flavours and clarity are the hallmarks of Jürgen Kissinger's dry Rieslings, Weissburgunder and Grauburgunder wines from Dienheim and Uelversheim. By appointment only.

Weingut Jean Buscher
Wormser Strasse 4
D 67595 Bechtheim
Tel: (06242) 872
Michael Buscher has made his name with daring, artist-label wines. Dry wines of solid quality from a wide range of grapes account for most of his production. Appointment recommended.

OPPENHEIM TO WORMS

Follow the B9 one kilometre south to Oppenheim. Its recorded history goes back to 765, when it was the property of Charlemagne. Work on the town's magnificent Gothic Katharinenkirche, with its unique red-stone *Langhaus* (Long House), began in the 13th century. Looking at the building today, you would not think that it suffered severe damage when Louis XIVs troops sacked and burned the town in 1689. The few other buildings that survived include part of the town wall and the nearby Rodensteiner Hof, today home to Oppemheim's leading producer, the Carl Koch estate. Parts of the *Hof* (manor) date back to the 14th century, and it is as worth a visit for its architecture as well as its powerful dry and dessert wines.

Powerful is definitely the right word to describe the wines from Oppenheim's best vineyards: the Sackträger, Schutzenhütte (a monopoly belonging to Louis Guntrum) and parts of the Herrenberg and Kreuz sites. They have heavy marl and chalky loam soils that give big, full-bodied wines. This style could hardly be in greater contrast to the wines from Nierstein's top sites. At present, Carl Koch, Dr Alex Senfter, Guntrum and Kühling-Gillot all make good examples, but nothing that can match Nierstein's best. Local Riesling does best on the marl soils, while Weissburgunder and Silvaner give the best results on chalky loam.

As you drive south out of Oppenheim on the B9, there is a fine view of the amphitheatre of vines centred upon the Sackträger. Continuing south from here, the B9 passes through a string of wine villages that also possess good vineyards. The first of these is Dienheim, where Brüder Dr Becker of neighbouring Ludwigshöhe produces some of

Right *The Liebrauenkirch, surrounded by the Liebfrauenstift-Kirchenstuck vineyard at Worms – it is from this vineyard that the original Liebfraumilch came.*

Left *Oppenheim and its Katharinenkirche, viewed from the Herrenberg vineyard. One would never guess at the troubled times in this church's history, from its imposing structure today.*

the best organic wines in the region from the local vineyards. The history of organic viticulture here goes back more than 30 years.

Ludwigshöhe, Guntersblum and Alsheim are villages with fine vineyards that yield quality wines at least equal those from Dienheim. However, the less well-known villages of Mettenheim and Bechtheim, approximately 10 kilometres north of Worms, and Uelversheim, five kilometres to the west of Guntersblum, have far more to offer. In Uelversheim, the best producers are Kissinger and Stallmann-Hiestand. Mettenheim is home to the Gerhard Sander estate, a pioneer of organic viticulture. The wine town of Bechtheim, nestling between vine-clothed hills, is one of the most attractive in all Rheinhessen. It can boast three good producers in Geil, Jean Bucher, and Christian Brenner. In nearby Westhofen, the Wittmanns also make good wines.

Worms is rightly famous for its *Dom*, or cathedral, one of the finest examples of late-Romanesque architecture in Europe. Its construction began under Bishop Burkhard and was completed in 1325; miraculously, it survived the destruction of the town in 1689, and then again in 1945. Less well-known, but hardly less-impressive is the Saint Pauluskirche, also begun during the early 11th century. For wine visitors, the Liebfrauenkirche to the north of the town centre is of greater significance. This Gothic masterpiece is surrounded by the Liebfrauenstift-Kirchenstück vineyard, from which the first Liebfraumilch wines were produced. Until well in to this century, they enjoyed an excellent international reputation. Only with the uncontrolled expansion of Liebfraumilch production during recent decades did the name become associated with quantity rather than quality. Today, the original vineyard is virtually a monopoly of the Heyl zu Herrnsheim estate of Nierstein.

Weingut Stallmann-Hiestand
Eisgasse 15
D 55278 Uelversheim
Tel: (06249) 8463
Dry-wine specialist Werner Hiestand concentrates on Rieslings, Silvaners and Weissburgunder wines. Quality is slightly erratic, but the best wines have plenty of body and character. By appointment only.

Weingut Wittmann
Mainzer Strasse 19
D 67593 Westhofen
Tel: (06244) 7042
Günter Wittmann is best-known for his clean, modern-style, dry white wines from a variety of grapes, but his dessert wines are no-less well-made. By appointment only.

Weingut Kühling-Gillot
Olmühlstrasse 25
D 55294 Bodenheim
Tel: (06135) 2333
Though situated just south of Mainz, this estate is well-known for its dry Rieslings from the top sites of Oppenheim. Often rather alcoholic, they cannot stand comparison with Roland Gillot's impressive dessert wines. Appointment recommended.

HOTELS

Dom-Hotel
Obermarkt 10
D 67547 Worms
Tel: (06241) 6913
Comfortable hotel in the centre of town, moderately priced.

RESTAURANTS

Rotisserie Dubs
Kirchstrasse 6
D 67550 Worms
Tel: (06242) 2023
In the Worms suburb of Rheindürkheim, Wolfgang Dubs mixes French, German and Asian influences to create the most sophisticated cuisine in Rheinhessen. Large as the list of German, French and Italian wines is, ask for alternative suggestions, as the cellars contain many unlisted wines.

RHEINHESSEN'S HILL COUNTRY

A glance at the map of Rheinhessen could easily give the impression that all the vineyards of the hill country yield similar wines, since the landscape seems to undulate in a relatively even manner.

However, this is far from being the case. A closer study of the region shows that the soils and microclimates vary considerably. The most recently planted vineyards here (from the late-1970s and early-1980s) are generally the poorest, occupying heavy soils upon which sugar-beet or potatoes once grew. Only inferior modern vine crossings such as Siegerrebe and Ortega, which ripen very early, make cultivation possible. They generally yield crudely aromatic wines of a kind that few people want to drink today.

However, scattered about the region, you can also find plantings of noble grapes such as Riesling and Weissburgunder, usually in vineyard sites on south-facing slopes. These will have been cultivated for centuries. In the past, viticulture automatically meant wealth, and the resulting affluence of the vineyard owners here invariably found expression in much more imposing architecture than is typical of simple farming villages.

The most important centre of quality wine production in Rheinhessen's hill country is the twin town of Flörsheim-Dalsheim. With its well-preserved medieval

RHEINHESSEN'S HILL COUNTRY

RECOMMENDED PRODUCERS

Weingut Keller
Bahnhofstrasse 1
D 67592 Flörsheim-Dalsheim
Tel: (06243) 456
Klaus and Hedwig Keller's estate is one of Rheinhessen's very best. Concentrated fruit, racy acidity and purity of aroma and flavour are the hallmarks of their excellent dry and dessert Rieslings. The Rieslaner and Huxelrebe dessert wines are hardly less impressive. Appointment recommended; essential Sundays.

Weingut Schales
Alzeyer Strasse 160
D 67592 Flörsheim-Dalsheim
Tel: (06243) 7003
Large estate with consistently high quality, run by brothers Heinrich, Arno and Kurt. Look for the very good, rich, dry Weissburgunders and the superb Huxelrebe dessert wines. Appointment recommended; essential Saturday afternoon and Sunday.

Sektkellerei Menger-Krug/ Krug'scher Hof
An der Königsmühle 7
D 55239 Gau-Ordenheim
Tel: (06733) 1337
The dry wines from the Krug'scher Hof are solidly made, but unremarkable, yet Regina and Klaus Menger-Krug's sparkling wines are among Germany's best. By appointment only.

Hedesheimer Hof
D 55271 Stadecken-Elsheim
Tel: (06136) 2487
Jürgen Beck's wines may not be the most powerful or sophisticated in Rheinhessen, but his dry Rieslings and Weissburgunders have plenty of ripe fruit and are well-made.

Weingut Göhring
Alzeyer Strasse 60
D 67592 Flörsheim-Dalsheim
Tel: (06243) 408
Wilfred Göhring's clean, fruity Rieslings with natural sweetness have attracted a good deal of attention during recent years. The other varieties are some way behind.

Right *Organic vineyards at the Heyl von Herrnsheim estate (Nierstein): alternate rows are left with grass cover to stabilize the vineyard's soil and to help retain its moisture.*
Above right *The Domdechaney and Steilwag vineyards – vines are not only grown on slopes in Germany, these have only gentle gradients.*

wall, it is also one of Rheinhessen's most beautiful towns. The best dry and dessert wines from the vineyards outside these walls are unquestionably among the entire region's finest wines. Keller and Schales are the quality leaders, followed by Göhring. Here Beerenauslese and Trockenbeerenauslese dessert wines produced from the Huxelrebe grape are an important speciality, combining intense, exotic and dried-fruit characters with a Riesling-like raciness and vitality. These wines can live for decades, thus proving that Flörsheim-Dalsheim's best wines are not merely pretenders making fraudulent claims to Rheinhessen's wine throne.

HOTELS

Hotel Krause
Gartenstrasse 2
55232 Alzey
Tel: (06731) 6181
Small, comfortable hotel with a pleasant restaurant serving good country cooking.

RESTAURANTS

Restaurant Weingewölbe
Hauptstrasse 32
D 67593 Bermersheim
Tel: (06244) 5242
In a vaulted cellar, Paul Bocuse's pupil Jean-Marie San Martin cooks in an unashamedly French style. Good local wines alongside French classics at friendly prices.

Restaurant La Maison de Marie
Weedengasse 8
D 55291 Saulheim
Tel: (06732) 3331
Marie-France Richard's French restaurant has a good reputation, but the food does not always live up to the high prices.

PLACES OF INTEREST

Alzey
Destroyed by Louis XIV's troops in 1689, the Schloss of Alzey was only restored at the beginning of this century. A range of wines from the town's vineyards can be tasted in its cellars. The Fischmarkt and Rossmarkt both have fine collections of half-timbered houses from the 16th to 18th centuries.

Below *Nierstein vineyards: these have done more than any other to make Rheinhessen wines famous, but there is space enough for poorer replicas to be grown.*

The Pfalz

You need to have a cold heart not to fall in love with the Pfalz at first sight. Its best vineyards lie on gentle inclines at the foot of the forested Haardt mountains, whose peaks not only provide a perfect backdrop for the region's numerous charming wine villages and towns, but also pick up most of the rain carried by westerly air-streams. This makes the Pfalz one of the driest, sunniest and warmest areas in Germany. Add in a diversity of generally light soils, and the result is an extremely wide range of exciting, dry, naturally sweet and dessert wines. Recently, some astonishingly sophisticated red wines have extended this palate of possibilities even further.

Once only a small area, centred around the town of Bad Dürkheim, was devoted to quality wine production, but during recent years there has been a growth in the number of exciting wines being produced throughout the region as a whole. It appears that the Pfalz's climate is particularly favourable for young, talented winegrowers. In almost every part of this large area, small family-owned estates are turning from the mass-production of everyday wines to quality winemaking. Nowhere else in Germany are there more exciting new producers than in the Pfalz.

Today it is Riesling that plays the most important role among the noble grapes cultivated here. In the region's top sites, the grape ripens fully in all but the poorest vintages, making possible more good, dry Riesling wines than anywhere else in Germany. It was during the 19th and early-20th centuries that the region established its international reputation, with Riesling wines that challenged those of the Rheingau. The pioneer was Andreas Jordan of Deidesheim, today the Dr von Bassermann-Jordan estate, which began selling vineyard-designated wines in 1802, and which harvested the first Auslese in the region in 1811. During the following decades, competition between the

Left *The warm, dry, sunny Pfalz region is currently experiencing a resurgence in winemaking with some of Germany's most exciting young producers making a stunning array of delicious, flavoursome wines.*

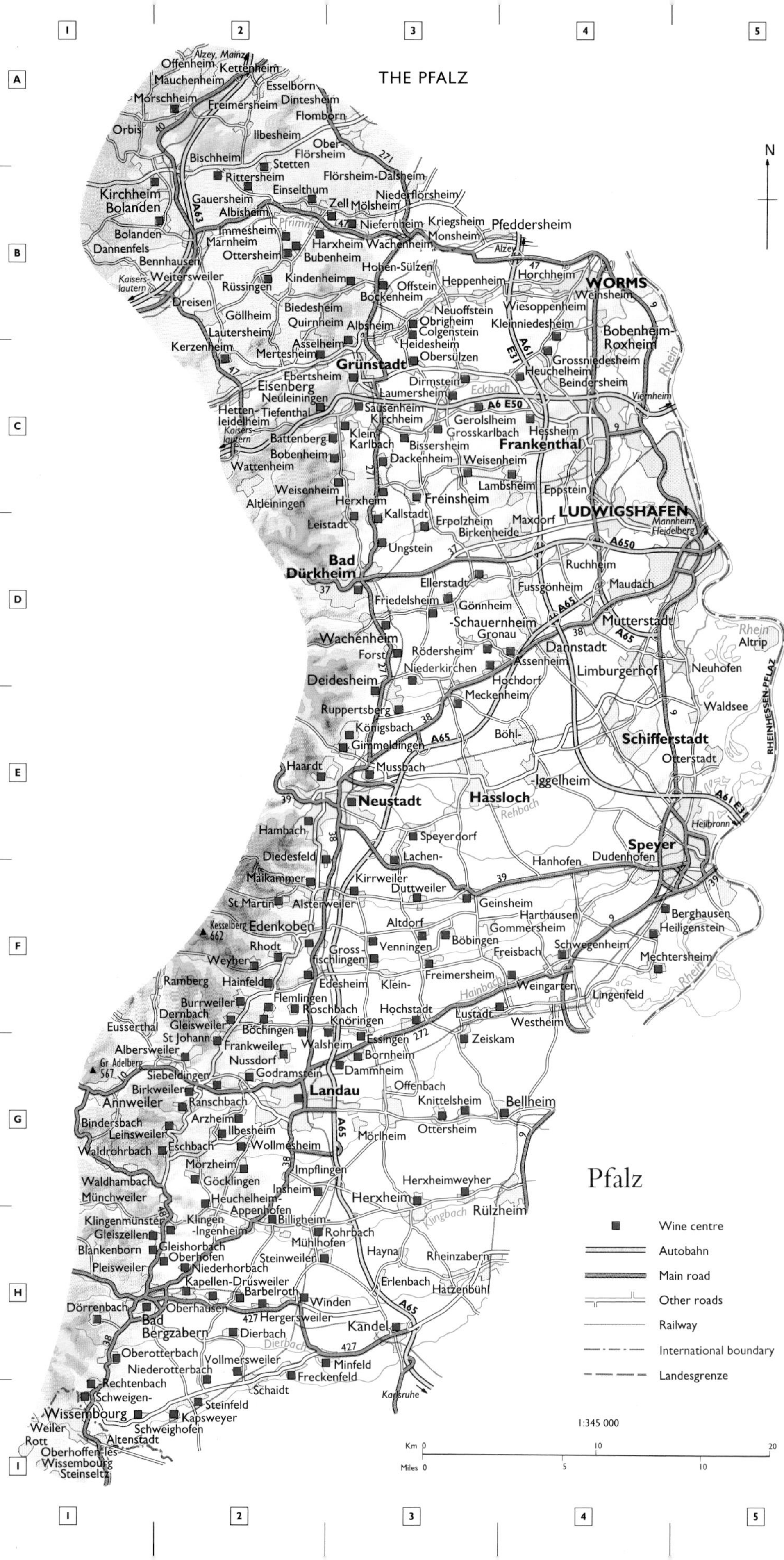
THE PFALZ
1
2
3
4
5
A
B
C
D
E
F
G
H
I
N
Alzey, Mainz
Offenheim
Kettenheim
Mauchenheim
Esselborn
Morschheim
Dintesheim
Freimersheim
Flomborn
Orbis
Ilbesheim
Ober-
Flörsheim
Bischheim
Stetten
Rittersheim
Flörsheim-Dalsheim
Kirchheim
Bolanden
Einselthum
Gauersheim
Niederflörsheim
Albisheim
Zell
Mölsheim
Pfrimm
Niefernheim
Kriegsheim
Pfeddersheim
Immesheim
Monsheim
Bolanden
Marnheim
Harxheim
Wachenheim
Alzey
Dannenfels
Ottersheim
Bubenheim
Bennhausen
Hohen-Sülzen
Kaiserslautern
Weitersweiler
Kindenheim
Offstein
Heppenheim
Horchheim
WORMS
Rüssingen
Bockenheim
Weinsheim
Dreisen
Biedesheim
Neuoffstein
Wiesoppenheim
Göllheim
Quirnheim
Albsheim
Obrigheim
Kleinniedesheim
Bobenheim-
Roxheim
Lautersheim
Colgenstein
Heidesheim
Kerzenheim
Asselheim
Mertesheim
Obersülzen
Grossniedesheim
Rhein
Grünstadt
Heuchelheim
Ebertsheim
Dirmstein
Beindersheim
Eisenberg
Laumersheim
Eckbach
Neuleiningen
Viernheim
Hettenleidelheim
Tiefenthal
Sausenheim
A6 E50
Kirchheim
Gerolsheim
Kaiserslautern
Battenberg
Klein-
Karlbach
Grosskarlbach
Hessheim
Bissersheim
Frankenthal
Bobenheim
Dackenheim
Weisenheim
Wattenheim
Lambsheim
Eppstein
Weisenheim
Herxheim
Freinsheim
Altleiningen
LUDWIGSHAFEN
Kallstadt
Leistadt
Erpolzheim
Maxdorf
Mannheim,
Heidelberg
Birkenheide
Ungstein
A650
Bad
Dürkheim
Ruchheim
Ellerstadt
Fussgönheim
Maudach
Friedelsheim
Gönnheim
-Schauernheim
Mutterstadt
Rhein
Altrip
Gronau
Dannstadt
Wachenheim
Forst
Rödersheim
Assenheim
Limburgerhof
Neuhofen
Niederkirchen
Deidesheim
Hochdorf
Meckenheim
Waldsee
RHEINHESSEN-PFALZ
Ruppertsberg
Königsbach
Böhl-
Schifferstadt
Gimmeldingen
Otterstadt
Haardt
Mussbach
-Iggelheim
Neustadt
Hassloch
Rehbach
A61 E31
Heilbronn
Hambach
Speyerdorf
Speyer
Diedesfeld
Lachen-
Hanhofen
Dudenhofen
Maikammer
Kirrweiler
Duttweiler
St Martin
Alsterweiler
Geinsheim
Berghausen
Harthausen
Kesselberg
662
Edenkoben
Altdorf
Gommersheim
Heiligenstein
Rhodt
Gross-
fischlingen
Venningen
Böbingen
Schwegenheim
Weyher
Freisbach
Mechtersheim
Rhein
Freimersheim
Ramberg
Hainfeld
Edesheim
Klein-
Weingarten
Hainbach
Lingenfeld
Flemlingen
Burrweiler
Roschbach
Hochstadt
Lustadt
Dernbach
Eusserthal
Gleisweiler
Knöringen
Westheim
Böchingen
St Johann
Walsheim
Essingen
Zeiskam
Frankweiler
Albersweiler
Nussdorf
Bornheim
Gr Adelberg
567
Dammheim
Siebeldingen
Godramstein
Offenbach
Birkweiler
Landau
Annweiler
Ranschbach
Knittelsheim
Bellheim
Arzheim
Bindersbach
Ottersheim
Leinsweiler
Ilbesheim
Mörlheim
Waldrohrbach
Eschbach
Wollmesheim
Mörzheim
Impflingen
Waldhambach
Göcklingen
Herxheimweyher
Insheim
Münchweiler
Heuchelheim-
Herxheim
Klingen
Appenhofen
Klingenmünster
-Klingen
Billigheim-
Rülzheim
Klingbach
-Ingenheim
Gleiszellen
Rohrbach
Blankenborn
Gleishorbach
Mühlhofen
Hayna
Oberhofen
Steinweiler
Rheinzabern
Pleisweiler
Niederhorbach
Kapellen-Drusweiler
Erlenbach
Hatzenbühl
Barbelroth
Winden
Dörrenbach
Oberhausen
Hergersweiler
Bad
Bergzabern
Dierbach
Kandel
Dierbach
Oberotterbach
Vollmersweiler
Minfeld
Niederotterbach
Freckenfeld
Rechtenbach
Schaidt
Karlsruhe
Schweigen-
Steinfeld
Wissembourg
Kapsweyer
Weiler
Schweighofen
Rott
Altenstadt
Oberhoffen-les-
Wissembourg
Steinseltz
A63
A61
E31
A65
40
47
271
9
37
38
39
272
427
Pfalz
Wine centre
Autobahn
Main road
Other roads
Railway
International boundary
Landesgrenze
1:345 000
Km 0
10
20
Miles 0
5
10

Bassermann-Jordan estate and those of Reichsrat von Buhl and Dr Bürklin-Wolf resulted in the region's leading trio earning the nickname 'The Three Bs'.

Many of the region's new star winemakers have made their reputations with dry wines from other grape varieties: Weissburgunder, Grauburgunder, Gewürztraminer, Muskateller or Scheurebe. These can pose serious competition to the best Pfalz Rieslings. In the dessert-wine field, Scheurebe can also match Riesling's achievements: both yield very lush, succulent wines that are rarely too massive or sweet. Spätburgunder makes the best red wines, while Dornfelder provides large quantities of simpler but appealing reds for everyday consumption.

A full appreciation of the Pfalz is not possible without sampling the local cooking; traditional cuisine is an inseparable part of the region's culture in a way that it is not in the Mosel or even the Rheingau. The substantial wines typical of the Pfalz work well with substantial dishes such as *Saumagen*, a pig's stomach stuffed with a mixture of pork, potatoes, herbs and spices, or blood sausage. These are not dishes not for the calorie-conscious or the faint-hearted, but they are dear to the region's inhabitants.

Below *A vineyard in Leistadt, just north of Bad Dürkheim in the Mittelhaardt. This area has some remarkable vineyards producing high quality Rieslings, yet the Mittelhaardt is charmingly unpretentious.*

BAD DURKHEIM

The natural place to begin a tour of the Pfalz is Bad Dürkheim. It is most easily reached from Ludwigshafen and Mannheim by the A650 Autobahn, which turns into the B37 shortly before reaching the town. In many ways, Bad Dürkheim reflects all the many facets of the Pfalz character. On the one hand, there are some grand old houses – for example, those housing the Fitz-Ritter and Karl Schaefer estates – and the elegant spa house; on the other, there are some ugly modern buildings and a pub housed in the world's largest barrel. Culture and kitsch alternate from one street to the next.

Likewise, Bad Dürkheim's vineyards range from some of the region's finest Riesling sites – the first-class Michelsberg and Spielberg – to large areas of flat ground that yield plain Müller-Thurgau whites and inspid Portugieser and Spätburgunder reds which are sold under the Durkheimer Feuerberg Grosslage name. Here you can find virtually all the grape varieties cultivated in the region, but – just as in the town itself – almost every facet of German wine from the sublime to the ridiculous.

These contrasting worlds collide at the town's *Wurstmarkt*, or sausage market, during the second half of September. This is more of a wine festival than a sausage celebration, with wines from large producers on offer. Those top producers in the area who do not have stands can often be seen mingling with the crowds. The Pfälzer do not share the sense of natural superiority that many

BAD DURKHEIM

RECOMMENDED PRODUCERS

Weingut Karl Schaefer
Weinstrasse Süd 30
D 67098 Bad Dürkheim
Tel: (06322) 2138
In the hands of talented winemaker Thorsten Rotthaus, the Schaefer estate has made a series of impressive dry wines that remain true to the traditional style of this excellent estate. Appointment recommended; closed Saturday afternoons and Sundays.

Weingut Pfeffingen-Fuhrmann-Eymael
Weinstrasse
D 67098 Bad Dürkheim
Tel: (06322) 8607
After a shaky period at the beginning of the 1990s, this highly regarded estate is back on form, making Rieslings that combine Pfalz richness with a Mosel-like elegance. Appointment recommended; essential Sundays.

Weingut Kurt Darting
Am Falltor 2
D 67098 Bad Dürkheim
Tel: (06322) 2983
After working at Müller-Catoir, Helmut Darting has rapidly established this young estate. Best are Ungsteiner Herrenberg Rieslings. Appointment recommended; essential Sundays.

Above and left *The vineyards of Bad Dürkheim vary greatly: some well-aspected sites yield high quality Riesling, other flatter, less scenic vineyards are the source other varieties such as Müller-Thurgau and Portugieser.*

Below *The Adler Inn in the centre of the attractive wine town of Freinsheim, one of the Pfalz's better kept secrets.*

Rheingauers have and they welcome every opportunity for a convivial glass of wine.

Just north of Bad Dürkheim on the B271 lies the cluster of buildings that is the tiny suburb of Pfeffingen. The eponymous estate is one of the Pfalz's leading Riesling producers, making the finest wines from the first-class Herrenberg vineyard of Ungstein; this is the impressive slope at whose foot the estate buildings stand. Ungstein itself is an unspectacular Pfalz wine village blessed with plenty of good vineyards.

Weingut Fitz-Ritter
Weinstrasse Nord 51
D 67098 Bad Dürkheim
Tel: (06322) 5389
Konrad and Alice Fitz run this substantial estate which specializes in very clean, modern-style Rieslings and Gewürztraminers. Appointment recommended; essential Saturday afternoon and Sunday.

Winzergenossenschaft Vier Jahreszeiten
Limburgstrasse 8
D 67098 Bad Dürkheim
Tel: (06322) 68011
Cooperative winery that is a reliable source of modestly priced white wines from a variety of grapes. Appointment recommended.

HOTELS

Kurparkhotel
Schlosspülatz 1
D 67098 Bad Dürkheim
Tel: (06322) 7970
A comfortable, stylish hotel in the centre of town, with sauna and indoor swimming pool.

Hotel Annaberg
Annaberg 1
D 67098 Bad Dürkheim
Tel: (06322) 2488
Once a famous wine estate, now a small, idyllically situated hotel. Towards Leistadt; ask for directions.

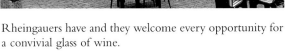

PLACES OF INTEREST

Hardenberg
The extensive ruins of the castle of Graf von Leiningen lie just outside Bad Dürkheim.

Seebach
The beautiful 12th-century Romanesque church of this small suburb of Bad Dürkheim has survived numerous wars.

NORTH OF BAD DURKHEIM

As you leave Ungstein travelling north on the B271, you'll pass the excavated remains of a Roman wine press on the left-hand side. It proves that the famous wine towns and villages of the Mittel Haardt are not the sole claimants to centuries of winegrowing tradition. Traditionally referred to as the Unter Haardt and regarded as capable of making only simple quaffing wines, this area actually produces some of the Pfalz's most exciting white and red wines.

The village of Kallstadt stands at the border of the Mittel Haardt and the Unter Haardt, and its great Saumagen vineyard provides some of the finest dry Rieslings in the whole of Germany. The vineyard is named after the dish due to a similarity of form (it is shaped rather like a sow's belly; *see* page 128); it was planted in an erstwhile limestone quarry. The heart of the Saumagen contains a few steep south-facing slopes, unusual in the area.

By chance, Saumagen wine makes a wonderful companion to the Saumagen dish, a partnership that can be experienced to perfection at Kallstadt's Weincastell restaurant, which features wines from the Koehler-Ruprecht estate. In recent years, this estate has proved that the soil, so reminiscent of that of Burgundy, can also yield remarkable Spätburgunder red wines. The best of these ought to make Burgundy's leading winemakers distinctly nervous. Weincastell and Koehler-Ruprechet are housed in an imposing half-timbered building. The idyllic courtyard at its centre is typical of the region's architectural traditions.

From Kallstadt, it is less than four kilometres to the attractive, walled town of Freinsheim, which contains a wealth of fine old houses. Beyond it lie the wine villages of Weisenheim am Sand, Grosskarlbach and Laumersheim, which are home to the Neckerauer, Lingenfelder and Knipser estates, respectively. They are all up-and-coming producers, Neckerauer and Lingenfelder specializing in white wine, and the Knipser brothers arguably the region's leading red wine producers. They have proven that Spätburgunder and Portugieser grapes are not the only ones

Upper Pfalz

BURGLAY Einzellage

First-class vineyard

Other vineyard

Woods

200 Contour interval 20 metres

Wine route

1:48 250

Km 0 1

Mile 0 ½

Above *Neuleiningen, one of the numerous picturesque villages which punctuate the fertile rolling landscape of the Pfalz.*

Below *Kallstadt marks the boundary between the Mittel Haardt and the Under Haardt and produces one of Germany's finest dry Rieslings and some extremely Burgundian Spätburgunder wines.*

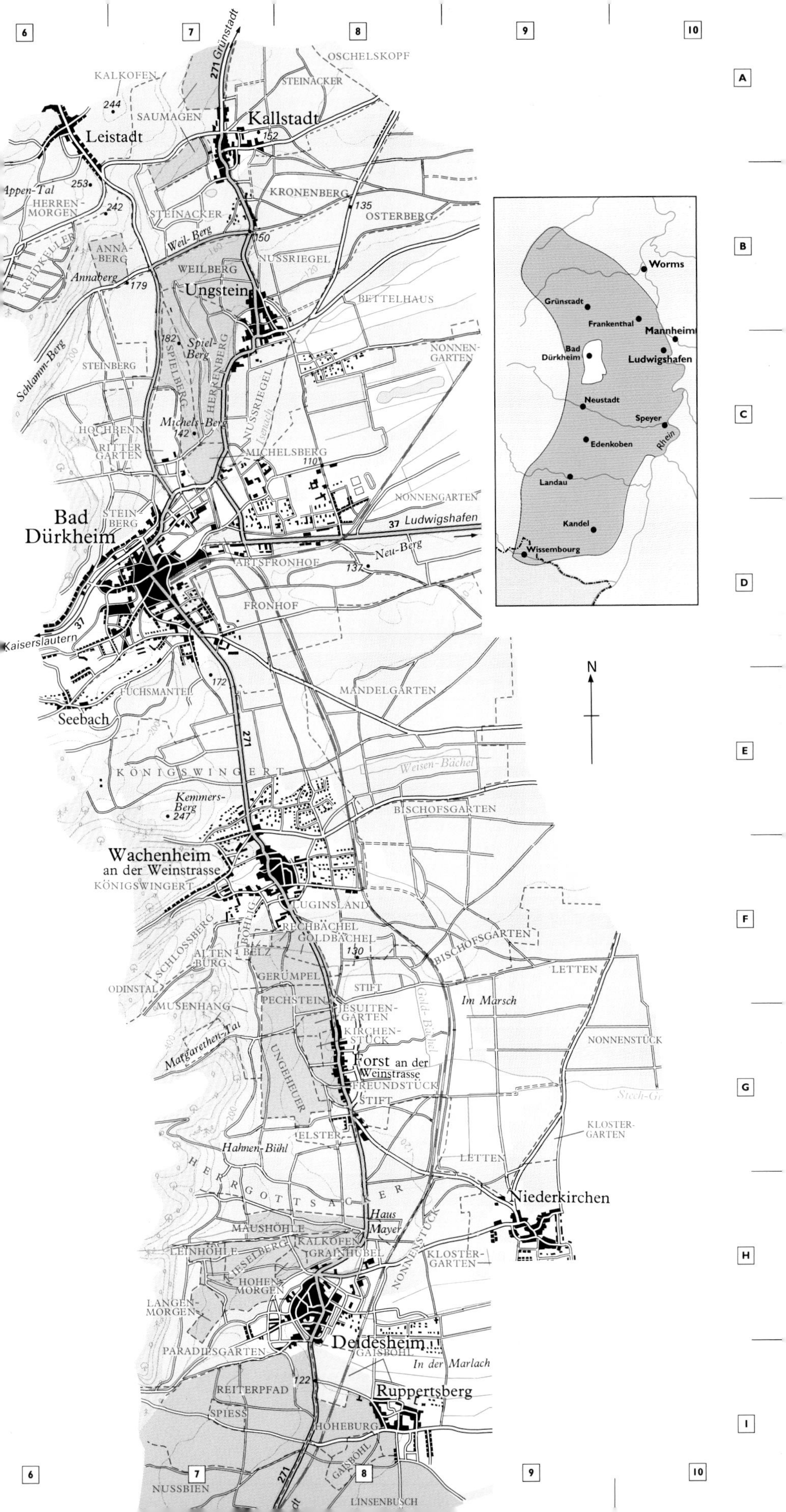

6
7
8
9
10
A
B
C
D
E
F
G
H
I
271 Grünstadt
OSCHELSKOPF
KALKOFEN
STEINACKER
244
SAUMAGEN
Kallstadt
Leistadt
152
Appen-Tal
253
HERREN-MORGEN
242
KRONENBERG
135
OSTERBERG
STEINACKER
Weil-Berg
150
KREIDKELLER
ANNA-BERG
NUSSRIEGEL
WEILBERG
Annaberg
179
Ungstein
BETTELHAUS
182
Spiel-Berg
NONNEN-GARTEN
Schlamm-Berg
STEINBERG
SPIELBERG
HERRENBERG
NUSSRIEGEL
Isenach
HOCHBENN
Michels-Berg
142
RITTER GARTEN
MICHELSBERG
110
NONNENGARTEN
Bad Dürkheim
STEIN-BERG
37 Ludwigshafen
ABTSFRONHOF
Neu-Berg
137
FRONHOF
37
Kaiserslautern
172
FUCHSMANTEL
MANDELGARTEN
Seebach
271
KÖNIGSWINGERT
Weisen-Bächel
Kemmers-Berg
247
BISCHOFSGARTEN
Wachenheim an der Weinstrasse
KÖNIGSWINGERT
LUGINSLAND
SCHLOSSBERG
BÖHLIG
RECHBÄCHEL
GOLDBÄCHEL
130
BISCHOFSGARTEN
ALTEN-BURG
BELZ
LETTEN
GERÜMPEL
ODINSTAL
STIFT
PECHSTEIN
Im Marsch
MUSENHANG
JESUITEN-GARTEN
Gold-Bächel
KIRCHEN-STÜCK
NONNENSTÜCK
Margarethen-Tal
Forst an der Weinstrasse
UNGEHEUER
FREUNDSTÜCK
STIFT
Stech-Gr
KLOSTER-GARTEN
ELSTER
Hahnen-Bühl
LETTEN
HERRGOTTSACKER
Niederkirchen
Haus Mayer
MAUSHÖHLE
NONNENSTÜCK
KALKOFEN
LEINHÖHLE
KIESELBERG
GRAINHÜBEL
KLOSTER-GARTEN
HOHEN-MORGEN
LANGEN-MORGEN
Deidesheim
PARADIESGARTEN
GAISBÖHL
In der Marlach
REITERPFAD
122
Ruppertsberg
SPIESS
HOHEBURG
GAISBÖHL
271
NUSSBIEN
LINSENBUSCH
Worms
Grünstadt
Frankenthal
Mannheim
Bad Dürkheim
Ludwigshafen
Neustadt
Speyer
Rhein
Edenkoben
Landau
Kandel
Wissembourg
N

NORTH OF BAD DURKHEIM

RECOMMENDED PRODUCERS

Weingut Koehler-Ruprecht
Weinstrasse 84, D 67169 Kallstadt
Tel: (06322) 1829
Arguably the greatest dry Rieslings in Germany; the finest Spätburgunder reds and sparkling wines in the Pfalz, too. By appointment only.

Weingut Knipser
Hauptstr 47, D 67229 Laumersheim
Tel: (06238) 742
Remarkable range of excellent red wines, and new-oak-aged whites. By appointment only; closed Sunday.

Weingut Lingenfelder
Hauptstr 27, D 67229 Grosskarlbach
Tel: (06238) 754
The best dry and dessert Rieslings and Scheurebes are opulent and expressive. Appointment recommended; closed Sundays.

Weingut Georg Henninger IV
Weinstrasse 93, D 67169 Kallstadt
Tel: (06322) 2277
Marvellous Weinstube that serves regional cooking (closed Mondays).

RESTAURANTS

Restaurant-Hotel Weincastell zum Weissen Ross
Weinstrasse 80-82, D 67169 Kallstadt
Tel: (06322) 5033
Offers a mix of Pfalz dishes and French-German classics. One of the most beautiful restaurants in the region. The hotel rooms are unpretentious and moderately priced.

Hotel-Restaurant Luther
Hauptstrasse 29, D 67248 Freinsheim
Tel: (06353) 2021
Dishes range from the sublime to the ridiculous. Unbeatable as a hotel.

Gebrüder Meurer
Hauptstr 67, D 67229 Grosskarlbach
Tel: (06238) 678
The place to eat outdoors during summer. The food is slightly variable in quality, but the list of local wines is excellent.

Restaurant Karlbacher
Hauptstr 57, D 67229 Grosskarlbach
Tel: (06238) 3737
Stunning half-timbered house with a small restaurant. Main courses are best.

WACHENHEIM AND FORST

RECOMMENDED PRODUCERS

Weingut Georg Mosbacher
Weinstrasse 27, D 67147 Forst
Tel: (06326) 329
Modern dry and dessert Rieslings packed with fruit, acidity and purity. Excellent value for money. Appointment recommended; essential Sundays.

to yield excellent reds; newcomers Dornfelder, Sankt Laurent and even Cabernet Sauvignon are finding some success here.

The vineyards lie between the steep slopes close to the Haardt forest and the flat arable land down on the plain. Vine-clothed, rolling hills are interspersed with fields and orchards, creating a quintessential Pfalz landscape. It is the very unpretentiousness of this area that is its charm; good wine and food are not difficult to find, but grandure and show are definitely in short supply.

WACHENHEIM AND FORST

Turn south from Bad Dürkheim onto the B271. The road takes you to some of the most famous wine towns and villages in the Pfalz.

The first of these is Wachenheim, a town that owes its fame to a single estate: Dr Bürklin-Wolf. From the 1920s through to the late 1970s, Dr Albert Bürklin-Wolf made many of the greatest Rieslings in the entire Pfalz, and the estate's Auslesen and higher Prädikat dessert wines from this period are legendary. The untiring dedication of its present director and co-owner, Christian von Guradze, has put the estate once again in the first rank of the region's wine producers.

It is not just with its wines that Bürklin-Wolf dominates Wachenheim. The estate's buildings set an imposing architectural accent in an otherwise rather dull setting. The cellars and offices are housed in a complex of classical buildings in the middle of Wachenheim on the right-hand side, while the Bürklin-von-Guradze family's imposing residence stands on the left as you leave town.

From here, there is a marvellous view over the best vineyards of Wachenheim, the wine village of Forst with its famous vineyards, and the church spire of Deidesheim protruding from behind vine-covered slopes in the background. The top sites of Wachenheim – the Gerümpel,

Goldbächel and Rechbächel (a monopoly run by Bürklin-Wolf) – lie to the right, behind and below the magnificent manor house of the Wolf estate. They yield Rieslings that combine intensity with classical elegance, rich peach and apricot fruit with subtle, minerally nuances. In addition to Bürklin-Wolf, the Josef Biffar estate of Deidesheim also makes first-class wines from these vineyards.

Forst is a complete contrast to its neighbour; its houses are strung out along a single cobbled street. The muted façades of the fine 16th- to 19th-century houses and the stillness of the entire place are distinctly reminiscent of the famous wine villages of Burgundy's Côtes d'Or. One of the oldest (and, unquestionably, the town's most picturesque) houses is the Förster Schlössel, home to the excellent Werlé estate. A short way along the street are Forst's other important producers: Georg Mosbacher, Eugen Müller, and Heinrich Spindler.

The graceful spire of Forst's church is the village's trademark, and the Kirchenstück and Jesuitengarten vineyards behind it are the twin sources of Forst's special reputation. These rather unimpressive-looking patches of well-tended vines can yield the most noble and majestic Rieslings in the region. This is primarily the result of what lies beneath the surface, ie a complex soil structure. Underneath the surface mixture of weathered sandstone and black bassalt stones lies a much heavier subsoil, which retains water throughout the hottest summers. This is the reason why, as early as 1830, the Bavarian Royal Surveyors office classified the Kirchenstück and Jeuitsengarten as the first- and second-best vineyards, respectively, in the Pfalz. During the recent reorganization of Forst's vineyards, enormous care was taken to preserve the distinctive features of this unique piece of land – something any visitor can appreciate during a walk through the cobbled lanes that wind between the town's famous vineyards.

Above *Spring in Forst, home to the Pfalz's two finest vineyards – Kirchenstück and Jesuitengarten.* Left *Schloss Wachenheim.*

Weingut Werlé Erben
'Förster Schlössel', Weinstrasse 84
D 67147 Forst
Tel: (06326) 8930
Beautifully crafted, traditional Rieslings: need time to reveal minerally depths. Appointments essential at weekends.

Weingut Dr Bürklin-Wolf
Weinstr 65, D 67157 Wachenheim
Tel: (06322) 8955
Sophisticated dry Rieslings; magnificent dessert wines. Tastings daily (except Sunday am); tours by appointment only.

Weingut Eugen Müller
Weinstrasse 34a, D 67147 Forst
Tel: (06326) 330
Rieslings from Kirchenstück vineyard belong to village's best. Appointment recommended; closed Sundays.

RESTAURANTS

Restaurant Lamm
Bismarkstr 21, D 67161 Gönnheim
Tel: (06322) 64330
Attractive restaurant in a fine old house serving regional food with flair.

Heinrich Spindler
Weinstrasse 44, D 67147 Forst
Tel: (06326) 280
Regional cooking and good Rieslings make this a popular Weinstube.

HOTELS

Hotel Goldbächel
Waldstr 99, D 67157 Wachenheim
Tel: (06322) 94050
Modern hotel with sauna in a quiet location close to the Haardt forest.

Right and below right *Wine production has been central to Deïdesheim for centuries; here it is demonstrated by an old vine growing in a courtyard and spectacular, immaculately tended vineyards.*

DEIDESHEIM

RECOMMENDED PRODUCERS

Weingut Josef Biffar
Niederkircher Strasse 13
D 67146 Deidesheim
Tel: (06326) 5028
With the support of Gerhard and Lilli Biffar, winemaker Ulrich Mell has made this estate the star of the Pfalz, producing brilliant dry and naturally sweet Rieslings from the best sites. Also makes an interesting dry medium-bodied Weissburgunder bottled *sur lie* straight from the yeast. By appointment only; closed Sundays.

Weingut Dr Deinhard/ Geheimrat J Wegeler Erben
Weinstrasse 10
D 67146 Deidehsiem
Tel: (06326) 221
Two estates sharing the same cellars, winemaker and administration. Heinz Bauer makes elegant, modern, dry Rieslings, and racy, crystal-clean Riesling dessert wines. Appointment recommended; closed Sundays.

Weingut Dr Ludwig von Bassermann-Jordan
Kirchgasse 10
D 67142 Deidesheim
Tel: (06326) 6006
Though not up to its past high standards, this large estate, committed 100% to the Riesling vine, remains a bastion of Pfalz wine culture. The best wines come from the top sites of Forst. Appointment recommended; closed weekends.

Weingut Reichsrat von Buhl
Weinstrasse 16
D 67146 Deidesheim
Tel: (06326) 96500
After a period of fluctuating quality, von Buhl is again making wines that are consistent in style and quality. However, they are still some way off top form. Appointment recommended.

Weingut Julius Ferdinand Kimmich
Weinstrasse 54, D 67142 Deidesheim
Tel: (06326) 342
The light, mostly dry wines are variable in quality, but the best offer good value for money. Appointment recommended; closed Sundays.

Weingut Georg Sieben
Weinstr 21, D 67143 Deidesheim
Tel: (06326) 214
Organic producer with rather austere dry wines of variable quality.

DEIDESHEIM

Deidesheim is rightly one of the most famous wine towns in the Pfalz. The high standing of its wines and the wealth they have brought during the last two centuries is reflected in the large 19th-century villas that stand at the town's edge. Entering by the B271 brings you past a row of these on the left-hand side. Continue towards the centre of town and on the right-hand side you'll pass the impressive estate houses of Dr Deinhard/Wegeler and Reichsrat von Buhl. The Marktplatz forms the heart of Deidesheim, with the Renaissance Rathaus, the frontage of the Hotel Deidesheimer Hof/Restaurant Schwarzer Hahn, and the late-Gothic church of Saint Ulrich.

While it is this scene that seems to remain most firmly imprinted in visitors' memories, the back streets of town also have much to offer. The complex of buildings that makes up the estate of Dr Bassermann-Jordan is a monument to the region's wine culture. As impressive as this architecture is, it is the subterranean architecture that most impresses. The recently deceased Dr Ludwig von Bassermann-Jordan amassed a great collection of Roman antiquities – primarily from local excavations and chance finds in the vineyards – which are now beautifully displayed in the estate's labyrinthine cellars.

On the other side of town lies the Josef Biffar estate, filled with a fascinating collection of German art from the late-19th century. Around the town's Schloss, which was rebuilt during the 18th century after being badly damaged by French troops in 1689, stand fragments of the town wall.

Deidesheim's wines are completely different from those of Forst; they are more extrovertly aromatic, richer and more succulent – and are thus archetypal Pfalz Rieslings. The best come from a group of small vineyard sites on the northwestern side of town, the Kalkofen, Grainhübel, Hohenmorgen, Langenmorgen and Leinhöhle being the finest of them. The generally light, local soils provide an advantage in that they warm quickly and are very free-draining. This means that Deidesheim's wines shine in wet years and can disappoint in hot years when drought-stress affects the vines. The recent reorganization of the town's vineyards, and consequent planting of new vines (which are vulnerable when young), has made drought stress a more common occurence than it was: greater vine age should help solve the problem. Currently the best wines are made by Josef Biffar, followed by Dr Deinhard, Dr von Bassermann-Jordan and von Buhl. Some work, however, needs to be done if the high overall standard which Deidesheim once maintained is to be achieved again.

RESTAURANTS

Restaurant Schwarzer Hahn/ Weinstube Saint Urban
Hotel Deidesheimer Hof
Am Marktplatz 1
D 67146 Deidesheim
Tel: (06326)
Manfred Schwarz's genius lies in his ability to refine classic regional dishes. In Schwarzer Hahn, this process is taken to a high point no other restaurant in the Pfalz can match. In St-Urban, the cooking is more traditional, but no less professional. The wine list is exceptional, offering a wide selection from the Pfalz, France, Italy and beyond. The fine hotel which houses both can also be highly recommended.

Gasthaus zur Kanne
Weinstrasse 31
67146 Deidesheim
Tel: (06326) 96600
Volker Frey's regional cooking with a sprinkling of classic dishes is rather hit and miss. The wine list offers a wide selection from owner Bürklin-Wolf, plus other top Pfalz producers and some serious French and Italian reds.

Above *Hambacher castle, which dates from the 11th century, is well worth visiting if only for the magnificent views it offers.*

RUPPERTSBERG TO NEUSTADT

RECOMMENDED PRODUCERS

Weingut Müller-Catoir
Mandelring 25
D 67433 Haardt
Tel: (06321) 2815
Winemaker Hans-Günther Schwarz has made this estate one of the top-10 producers in the whole of Germany. Explosively aromatic, rich, concentrated wines in every style, from light and dry up to opulent dessert wines from a wide range of grapes; Riesling, Scheurebe and Rieslaner are particularly strong. Nevertheless, good value for money. Appointment only; closed weekends.

Weingut Bergdolt
Klostergut Sankt Lamprecht
D 67435 Duttweiler
Tel: (06327) 5027
Rainer Bergdolt makes astonishing rich, intense Weissburgunder with the stature of Meursault. Recently he has added impressive, new-oak-aged Chardonnay and rich Pinot Noir reds to the range. Appointment recommended; closed Sundays.

RUPPERTSBERG TO NEUSTADT

The charming village of Ruppertsberg lies only a kilometre outside Deidesheim. Its wines may not often be quite as fine as those from the villages further north, but it more than compensates for this by producing large quantities of reasonable-quality wine.

This is the result of being a large area with favourably exposed vineyards and generally light soils. The vineyards to the west of the B271, particularly the Reiterpfad and Nussbein sites, yield richer, slower-developing wines. In contrast, wines from the vineyards on the eastern side of the road are lighter and charmingly approachable from an earlier stage in their development. 'Pretty' would be a good word to describe the Ruppertsberg wines. Because of their comparatively lowly position in the local vineyard hierarchy, they often represent very good value for money. The best sources are Josef Biffar and Dr Bürklin-Wolf

Königsbach lies to the west of the B271, and has long enjoyed a good reputation for wines from the Idig site, which are more powerful and better-structured than typical Ruppertsbergers. Today, the Christmann estate of Gimmeldingen is the sole standard-bearer for this vineyard. Likewise, the vineyards between Mussbach, Gimmeldingen and Neustadt have been made famous by a single wine estate: Müller-Catoir. Like the top sites of Forst, these vineyards do not look particularly remarkable, though the view from the road up towards Gimmeldingen, which nestles below Haardt, has an undeniable charm.

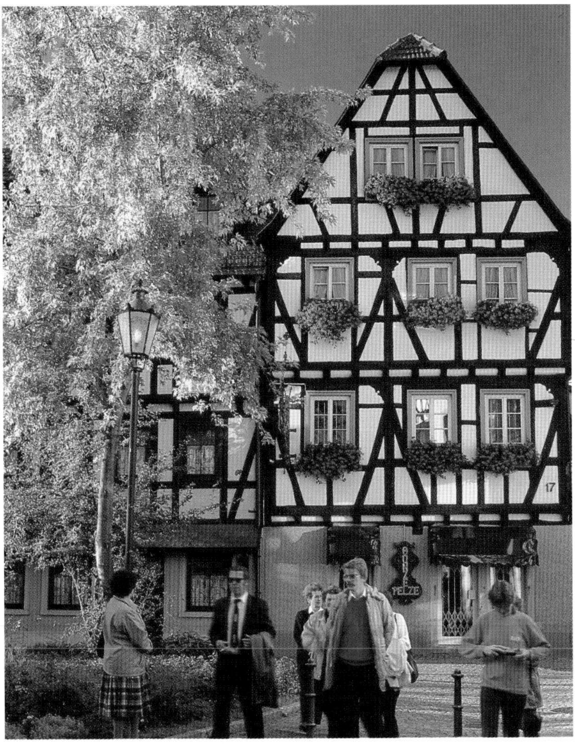

Left *One of the many 16th and 17th-century buildings that dominate the centre of Neustadt, despite some ugly modern developments on the town's outskirts.*
Below *This gateway dated 1594 reveals Deidesheim's long history as a source of fine wines.*

The main contributer to the high quality of the local wines is the 553-metre peak of the Weinbiet, directly to the east, in whose rain-shadow the vineyards stand. Its shade results in wines with considerable richness, body and aroma. In the hands of Müller-Catoir's winemaking genius, Hans-Günther Schwarz, masterpieces are frequently the end product. The estate lies in the pretty village of Haardt, indicated by the sign on the right-hand side of the road when entering Neustadt along the B271.

Although the approach to Neustadt – literally, 'new town' – is tainted by some ugly modern developments at the edge of town, the centre is dominated by old buildings, with numerous houses from the late-16th and early-17th centuries. It is worth taking time to explore this architectural treasure-trove. Just to the south of Neustadt lies the semi-ruined castle of Hambach, parts of which date back to around 1100. It is as much worth a visit for the fine views of the surrounding countryside as it is for the architecture.

Not far from Hambach (take the B39 towards Speyer) lies the village of Duttweiler, officially a suburb of Neustadt, although it is situated eight kilometres from the town centre. This is the home of the ex-monastic property of Klosterhof Sankt Lamprecht, which is now owned by the Bergdolt family. The Bergdolt's wine estate makes the finest dry Weissburgunder in the Pfalz from old vines in the Mandelberg site – it is untraditional, but a visit here is a fitting way in which to end any tour of the Mittelhaardt.

Weingut Christmann
Peter-Koch-Strasse 43
D 67435 Gimmeldingen
Tel: (06321) 66039
Since the late 1980s, Steffen Christmann's dry Rieslings from Gimmeldingen and Ruppertsberg have gained in depth and elegance. Appointment recommended; essential on Sundays.

Weingut am Burggarten (Geissler)
Burggarten 7
D 67435 Duttweiler
Tel: (06327) 2770
Slightly rustic, dry Weissburgunder, Grauburgunder and Silvaner with plenty of character. Appointment only.

Winzerverein Hoheburg
D 67152 Ruppertsberg
Tel: (06326) 6035
Reliable cooperative with light, aromatic Rieslings. Appointment recommended.

HOTELS

Page-Kongresshotel
Exterstrasse 2
D 67433 Neustadt
Tel: (06321) 8980
Comfortable, modern hotel in the centre of Neustadt. Slightly soulless, but well-run.

RESTAURANTS

Restaurant Mandelhof
Mandelring 11
D 67433 Haardt
Tel: (0321) 88220
Pleasant restaurant with competent, if slightly pretentious, cuisine. Also attractive hotel rooms. Just a few doors from Müller-Catoir.

SOUTHERN PFALZ

RECOMMENDED PRODUCERS

Weingut Okonomierat Rebholz
Weinstrasse 54
D 76833 Siebeldingen
Tel: (06345) 3439
Hans-Jörg Rebholz continues the family tradition for producing racy, dry Rieslings. Weissburgunder, Grauburgunder, Gewürztraminer and Muskateller of great sophistication dominate. The tannic Spätburgunder reds are also very good.
By appointment only.

Weingut Herbert Messmer
Gaisbergstrasse 132
D 76835 Burrweiler
Tel: (06345) 2770
The new star of the southern Pfalz, thanks to the dedication of Gregor Messmer. The excellent dry and dessert Rieslings from the slate soil of the first-class Schäwer site are both racy and minerally. Also very good dry Weissburgunder, naturally sweet Scheurebe, and Sankt-Laurent reds. Appointment recommended; closed Sundays.

Weingut Dr Wehrheim
Südliche Weinstrasse 8
D 76831 Birkweiler
Tel: (06345) 3542
Karl-Heinz Wehrheim makes the richest, most succulent dry Rieslings, Weissburgunder and Grauburgunder in the Southern Pfalz. During the last few years, his Spätburgunder red wines have improved in leaps and bounds. Appointment recommended.

Above *This ornate sign indicates the entrance to the wine village of Flemlingen near Landau.*
Right *The Haardt mountains (here near Albersweiler) protect the Pfalz from too much cloud and rain.*

SOUTHERN PFALZ AND SPEYER

The Southern Pfalz, also known as the *Ober Haardt* (Upper Haardt), *Südliche Weinstrasse* (southern wine road) or ironically the *Süssliche* Weinstrasse (*sweet* wine road) does not have a great tradition of quality wine production. During the 1960s and 1970s, its winegrowers and cooperatives jumped on the sweet-wine bandwagon and pumped out huge volumes of wishy-washy wines with little or no character. However, during this period, the first top-class dry and dessert wines were already being produced by the Rebholz estate of Siebeldingen and Dr Wehrheim in nearby Birkweiler (both just to the west of Landau). The movement set an example that was followed by more and more of their colleagues. Today, the best wines from the southern Pfalz equal and excel those from further north.

The natural beauty of the Southern Pfalz is abundant. Here, the Haardt mountains are more jagged and irregular than around Bad Dürkheim and Neustadt, sometimes sculpted by millenia of erosion into forms reminiscent of Chinese landscape prints and paintings. The comparative scarcity of tourists compared to the Deidesheim area means that this is an excellent place to seek complete peace. Only the towns of Landau and Bad Bergzabern ever approach

anything hectic, and the numerous picturesque wine villages provide ample sources of diversion. The most famous – and arguably the most attractive – of these is Saint Martin, just eight kilometres south of Neustadt.

The first exciting wines appear half-a-dozen villages further south in Burrweiler, which seems to be little-known in spite of its 18th-century castle and many fine old houses. The Herbert Messmer estate makes superb Rieslings from the only vineyard in the Pfalz with a grey-slate soil: the first-class Burrweiler Schäwer. These wines face serious competition from the Rieslings from the Birkweiler Kastanienbusch, whose red-slate soil yields similarly elegant and refined wines. This is excellent Weissburgunder and Grauburgunder country, both grapes yielding extremely good, dry wines that combine substance and freshness. Gewürztraminer and Muskateller are traditional specialities. There are several pockets of fine quality south of here, the most important being the vineyards of Schweigen, right next to the border with Alsace. Here, the Spätburgunder grape yields full-bodied, richly textured wines, particularly in the hands of Fritz Becker.

No tour of the Pfalz would be complete without a visit to Speyer. Together with the cathedral of Worms, Speyer's

Weingut Friedrich Becker
Hauptstrasse 29, D 76889 Schweigen
Tel: (06342) 290
Spätburgunder specialist Fritz Becker sells new-oak-aged red wines as *Tafelwein* (table wine), the traditional-style wines (from old wooden casks) as QbA or Spätlese Trocken. High general standard. By appointment only.

Weingut Münzberg
D 76829 Landau-Godramstein
Tel: (06341) 60935
Brothers Gunter and Rainer Kessler are rightly best-known for the powerful, but precisely balanced dry wines from the Weissburgunder and Grauburgunder grapes. Appointment recommended; closed Sundays.

Weingut Bernhart
Hauptstrasse 8
D 76889 Schweigen
Tel: (06342) 7202
Up-and-coming red-wine specialist making rich, stylish Spätburgunders with refined oaky nuances, and prices to match. Unremarkable white wines. By appointment only; closed Sundays.

Weingut Siegrist
Am Hasensprung 4
D 76829 Leinsweiler
Tel: (06345) 1309
Although white grapes dominate, it is the Spätburgunder and Dornfelder reds that stand out. Appointment recomended; essential Sundays.

RESTAURANTS

Hotel-Restaurant Zur Krone/ Pfälzer Stuben
Hauptstrasse 62–64
D 76863 Hayna
Tel: (07276) 50810
Karl-Emil Kuntz's cuisine is unashamedly elaborate and refined. Everything from the terrines to the venison shows creativity and craftsmanship of the highest standard. Allow plenty of time to appreciate Zur Krone properly, or try Kuntz's impressive interpretation of the Pfalz's regional cooking in the Pfälzer Stuben. The hotel rooms are modern and comfortable.

Restaurant Sonnenhof
Mühlweg 2
D 76833 Siebeldingen
Tel: (06345) 3311
A pleasant, relaxed restaurant where tourists mingle with locals. Mathias Goldberg and Volker Krug's cooking is competent and unpretentious.

Zehntkeller
Weinstrasse 5
D 76829 Leinsweiler
Tel: (06345) 3075
Neither food nor wine may rise above the most rustic level, but the ambience is extraordinary.

**Hotel Binshof bei den Seen/
Restaurant Salierhof**
Binshof 1
D 67346 Speyer
Tel: (06332) 6470
This new hotel and restaurant has been created at great expense. Chef Klaus Walter has rapidly earned a high reputation for an original mix of regional cooking (Pfalz and French) and *haut cuisine*. The hotel rooms are comfortable and modern.

PLACES OF INTEREST

Bad Bergzabern
This attractive town close to the border with Alsace has many fine buildings, including the Renaissance Herzögliches Schloss and Gasthaus zum Engel.

Edenkoben
The Villa Ludwigshöhe houses German Post-Impressionist painter Max Slevogt's extensive collection of paintings, sculptures and drawings, and lies just to the west of Edenkoben. From here, a cable-car runs to the ruined Rietburg castle, which offers magnificent views of the surrounding countryside.

Leinsweiler
A beautiful old village full of minor architectural masterpieces, of which the Renaissance Rathaus of 1619 is the most important. Schlossgut Neukastell above Leinsweiler was the home of painter Max Slevogt.

The southern Pfalz is ideal for a peaceful break due to the general lack of tourists, but is full of wine villages such as Ranschbach (above).

is one of the great Romanesque monuments of Europe. The cathedral's foundation stone was laid in 1030, and most of the building dates from the 11th to 13th centuries, although the town had been a bishophric since the seventh century; there was probably a bishop here even during the late-Roman period. Its crypt is the resting-place of eight German kings. Close by stand fragments of the town wall, which, together with the Dom, were all that remained of Speyer when the French troops left in 1689. The nearby Baroque *Dreifaltigkeitskirche* (Church of the Holy Trinity) of 1717 is hardly less worthy of note, particularly for its painted wooden interior. The Historisches Museum der Pfalz has become one of the nation's leading museums, staging special exhibitions of the highest international standards. It is also home to the Pfalz's fine wine museum.

Left *Burrweiler produces some of the southern Pfalz's finest Rieslings from the Burrweiler Schäwer vineyard – the reason they are so good lies in the red slate soil which resembles that of parts of the Mosel. The word* Schäwer *actually means slate in the local dialect.*

Below *The other source of fine Rieslings in the southern Pfalz is the town of Birkweiler. The best vineyards have an altitude of around 300 metres and are close to the forest which provides shelter.*

GLOSSARY

Anbaugebiet – literally 'region of origin'. Germany has 13 winegrowing regions
Auslese – traditionally rich, naturally sweet wine made from selected late picked grapes, but today the German wine law defines the category in purely analytic terms. Some of these wines are now vinified dry (see Trocken and Halbtrocken)
Autobahn – the German motorway. Still without tolls or speed limits (except where signs indicate otherwise!)
Bach – a small stream, sometimes incorporated in to vineyard names, eg the Goldbächel of Wachenheim/Pfalz
Bäckerei – a bakery, which in Germany means a source of real bread, an essential part of the survival kit for any wine tour
Barrique – small oak cask, most commonly of 225 or 300 litres of French or local wood used for the fermentation and/or maturation of red and white wines. Until recently German 'Barrique-Weine' were usually too oaky, but some fine examples are now being made
Beerenauslese – extremely rich, luscious wine produced from shrivelled, botrytis-affected berries (see Edelfäule). If made from Riesling or other noble grapes rare and expensive
Bundesstrasse – main highways, each of which has a number that appears on roadsigns. Unless indicated otherwise the speed limit is 100 kilometers per hour
Burg – a fortified tower or keep
Dom – a cathedral (see Münster)
Edelfäule – noble rot. Most of the great German dessert wines are produced from grapes affected by this fungus (*Botrytis cinerea*)
Edelstahl – stainless steel, the modern alternative to wood for the construction of wine casks
Eiswein – ice wine, made from grapes picked whilst frozen
Erzeugerabfüllung – literally 'bottled by the producer', which today usually means by a cooperative (see Gutsabfüllung and Winzergenossenschaft)
Federweisse – fermenting wine sold during the harvest period. Milky in appearance and yeasty in flavour it is traditionaly drunk with onion tart
Filtration – all German white wines are filtered before bottling, an essential operation to gaurantee their stability. Some top German reds are now bottled unfiltered
Fuder – the traditional 1,000 litre oak barrel used in the Mosel-Saar-Ruwer since Roman times
Gärung – fermentation, which in Germany can last anything from a few days to six months
Gutsabfüllung – estate-bottled (see Erzeugerabfüllung)
Halbtrocken – legal designation for wines that are just off dry. Depending on the grape and region these can either taste completely dry or quite sweet
Hectare (ha) – measure of area, approximately 2.47 acres
Hectolitre – measure of volume, 100 litres
Hefe(brand) – spirit distilled from the lees left after fermentation, usually water white and softer than Trester
Jahrgang – the vintage
Kabinett – traditionally the lightest German wines with alcohol levels that can go as low as 7 degrees in the Mosel-Saar-Ruwer, but law sadly sets no maximum alcohol limit
Keller – the cellar
Kellerei – a company which buys, blends and bottles wine, the equivalent of a *négociant* in France
Kelterhaus – the press house
Kirche – a church
Lage – an individual vineyard site or 'Einzellage'. Unfortunately the names of 'Grosslage', or collective sites which cover much larger areas, read like Einzellage names
Land – Germany is a federation of states , or 'Lände'. Not to be confused with Anbaugebiete, or winegrowing regions
Landwein – sub-category of Table Wine (see Tafelwein) for dry, normally cheap, quaffing wines
Lees – the dead yeast that settles to the bottom of the cask after fermentation
Lese – the harvest
Lieblich – designation for wines with natural sweetness that appears on price lists, but almost never on labels
Markt – a market or marketplace
Metzger – a butcher, often also selling ham and sausage (see Schinken and Wurst)
Most – freshly pressed grape juice
Münster – a minster, or cathedral
Oechsle – measure of the grape sugar content. The German wine law classifies the nation's wines solely on the basis of grape sugar content
Offene Weine – wines available in restaurants and bars to buy by the glass
Pfifferlinge – chanterelle mushrooms, an important speciality during the summer months
Qualitätswein (QbA) – legal designation for wines which have been chaptalized (ie to which sugar has been added during the fermentation to increase the alcoholic content)
Rathaus – the town hall
Säure – acidity, a vital consituent of German white wines. It is usually measured in gramms per litre of tartaric acid, but analytical figures are little guide to taste or quality
Schatzkammer – rarities, or library cellar
Schinken – ham, which may be cooked, dried or smoked
Schnitzel –a steak; unless the menu says otherwise it will almost certainly be pork. A cliché of German cooking
Schloss – usually translated as castle, but actually a palace rather than a set of fortifications
Schînung – fining, or the addition of substances to young wines to aid their clarification. Whilst France's top vintners prefer to fine rather than filter young wines, most of Germany's top quality wines are lightly filtered, but unfined
Sekt – sparkling wine
Spargel – asparagus, an important speciality during the months of April, May and June. In Germany, it is usually white and served as a main dish, accompanied by ham or a small steak
Spätlese – traditionally a late-harvested wine with some natural sweetness. Today the law sets disgracefully low minimum standards for this category, and only examples from reputable growers will be something special
Spitzenlage – a top vineyard site, today often referred to as 'Grand Cru'
Steillage – a steeply sloping vineyard site
Steinpilze – the German name for cäpes or porcini mushrooms, an important speciality during the summer and early autumn
Stück – the oval, 1,200 litre casks used in the Rhine Valley since at least the Middle Ages
Sulphur dioxide – an antioxidant used in all wine; harmless, but sometimes detectable in very young wines
Tafelwein – Table Wine
Trester (brand) – the German name for marc or grappa, a spirit distilled from the grape skins left after pressing, often as rough as its foreign cousins
Trocken – the legal designation for dry wines
Trockenbeerenauslese – the pinnacle of Germany's legal wine classification system. Extremely rich, super-luscious wines made from raisin-like shrivelled berries. If made from Riesling or other noble grapes very rare and extremely expensive
Vietel(e) – a quarter litre glass of wine
Weinberg – a vineyard
Weingut – a wine estate
Winzergenossenschaft – a winemaking co-operative
Wurst – sausage, which comes in a thousand forms, cooked and cured

INDEX

Indexer's note: Towns are given in brackets for hotels and restaurants.

GAZETTEER

PICTURE CREDITS

Front Jacket: Pictor International
Back Jacket: Tony Stone Images/John Wyand

Cephas Picture Library /**Nigel Blythe** 68/69, 80, 90 bottom, 97 top, 106, 116/117, 121, 131 bottom, 138, 139 top, /**David Burnett** 108, 114, 115 top, 125 top, /**Andy Christodolo** 76/77, 81, 84, 86, 124, 126/127, 128, 131 top right, 132 bottom, 132 top, /**Mick Rock** 6, 78 top, 82, 85, 87, 88/89, 93 top, 96/97, 104/105, 107 bottom, 107 top, 112/113, 118, 120 top, 122, 123, 134, 136, 137, 139 bottom, 140/141, 142/143.
Armin Faber/ 5 centre bottom, 5 top centre, 8/9, 10, 11, 12/13 bottom, 14/15, 16/17, 18/19, 20/21, 29 top right, 29 bottom, 31 bottom, 38/39, 40/41 top, 43 top right, 45, 46/47, 48/49, 53, 54/55, 56, 57, 58/59, 61, 62, 64/65, 66/67, 72/73, 74, 75, 77 top, 78 bottom, 83, 90 top, 91, 93 bottom, 95, 100 bottom, 101 bottom, 102/103, 110, 111, 115 bottom, 117 top, 125 bottom, 127 top, 130/131, 135
Scope /**Charles Bowman** 69 top, /**Jacques Guillard** 3, 5 top, 5 bottom, 9 top, 22/23, 24/25, 25 right, 26, 28/29 top, 31 top, 32, 33, 34, 35, 36/37, 38 bottom left, 41 bottom right, 42/43 bottom, 52, 55 top right, 60, 63, 70, 71, 89 top, 92, 94, 97 bottom right, 100 top, 101 top.